Peter's Tomb Recently

Discovered In Jerusalem

Peter's Tomb
Recently Discovered
In Jerusalem

F. Paul Peterson

Copies may be obtained from the publisher,

F. Paul Peterson

~~P. O. Box 568, McKeesport, Pa.~~

2520

P. O. BOX ~~2884~~, FORT WAYNE, IND.

PRICE $1.00

Table Of Contents

CHAPTER ONE

Peter's Tomb

While visiting a friend in Switzerland, I heard of what seemed to me to be the greatest discovery since the time of Christ — that Peter was buried in Jerusalem and not in Rome. The source of this rumor, written in Italian, was not clear; and it left considerable room for doubt, or rather wonder. Rome was the place where I could investigate the matter; and if such proved encouraging, a trip even to Jerusalem might be necessary in order to gather valuable first-hand information on the subject. I therefore went to Rome. After talking to a number of priests and investigating various possible sources of information, I finally was greatly rewarded by learning where I could buy the only known book on the subject, which was written in Italian. It is called Gli Scavi del "Dominus Flevit," printed in 1958 at the Tipografia dei PP. Francescani in Jerusalem. It was written by P. B. Bagatti and J. T. Milik, both Roman Catholic priests. The story of the discovery was there, but it was purposely hidden and much was lacking, it seemed to me. I consequently determined to go to Jerusalem to see for myself, if possible, that which seemed to me almost unbelievable, especially since it came from priests, who naturally, from existing ideas concerning the tomb of Peter, would be the last ones to welcome such a discovery or to bring it to the attention of the world.

7

In Jerusalem, I spoke to many Franciscan priests, who all agreed that the bones of Simon Bar Jona (St. Peter) were found in Jerusalem, on the Mount of Olives, on the Franciscan monastery site, called "Dominus Flevit" (meaning "Jesus Wept"). The pictures, which I had a photographer take, show the story. The first shows an excavation where the names of Christian Biblical characters were found written on bone boxes. The names of Mary and Martha were found on one bone box, and right next to it was one with the name of Lazarus, their brother, written on it. Other names of early Christians were found on other boxes. Of greatest interest, however, was that which was found within twelve feet from the place where the bones of Mary, Martha, and Lazarus were found — the remains of St. Peter. They were found in a bone-box, on the outside of which was clearly and beautifully written in Aramaic, "Simon Bar Jona."

I talked to the Yale professor, Marvin Pope, who is an archeologist, and is director of the American School of Oriental Research in Jerusalem. He told me that it would be very improbable that a name with three words, and one so complete, could refer to more than one person, St. Peter. But what makes the possibility of error more remote is that the remains were found in a Christian burial ground, and more yet, of the first century, the very time in which Peter lived. All this makes it virtually impossible that the inscription "Simon Bar Jona" could refer to any other than St. Peter.

I talked to the co-writer of this Italian book on the subject, Priest Milik. In the presence of my friend, a Christian Arab, Mr. S. J. Mattar, who is the warden of the Garden Tomb, where Jesus was buried and rose again, Priest Milik admitted that he knew that the

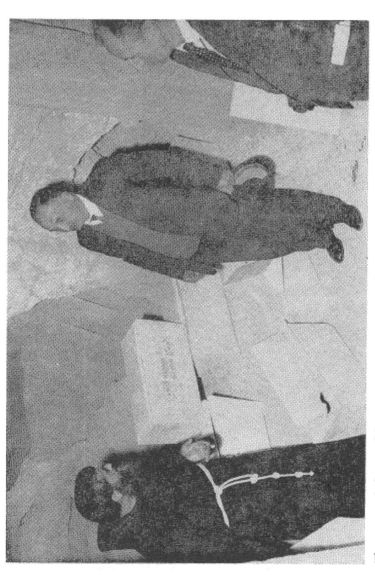

The scene of the sepulcher on Mount of Olives where the bones of St. Peter and other early Christians were found.

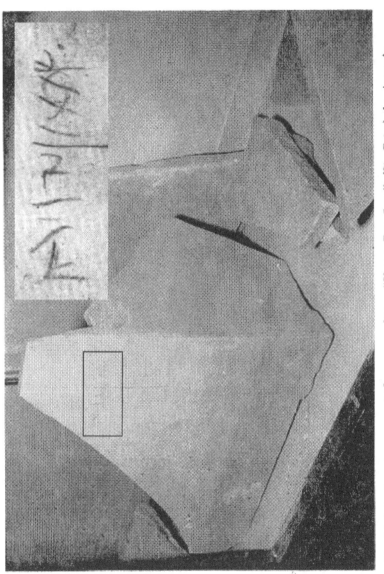

On this bone-box, or ossuary, is the name written, "Simon Bar Jona" (St. Peter) in Aramaic.

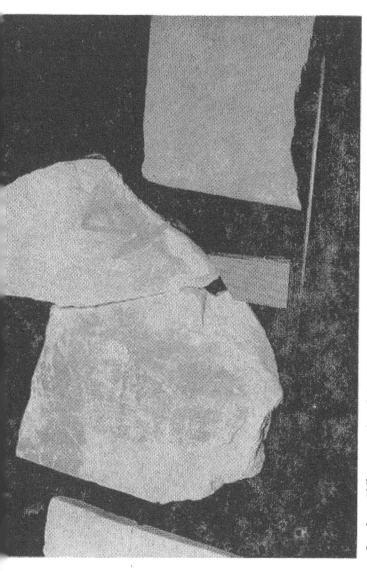

On the middle stone, found in this excavation, one sees a mark which is the first two letters of the Greek word which means Christ.

Left to right: Mr. S. J. Mattar, the author, and priest J. T. Milik. The priest confirming the inscription of "Simon Bar Jona," in this book, mentioned herein, of which he is co-writer.

bones of St. Peter are not in Rome, and he agreed with me that there are a hundred times more evidence that Peter was buried in Jerusalem than in Rome. I have spoken to many Franciscan priests on the subject, who were or had been in Jerusalem, and they all agreed that the tomb and remains of St. Peter are in Jerusalem. There was just one exception, which only proved the point. The Franciscan priest, Augusto Spykerman, who was in charge of the semi-private museum located inside the walls of old Jerusalem, by the site of the Franciscan Church of the Flagellation, was that exception. When I asked to see the museum, he showed it to Mr. Mattar, a professional photographer and me, but he told us nothing of the discovery. I knew that the evidence of Peter's burial was there, for priests had told me that relics from the burial were preserved within this museum. People who lived in Jerusalem all their lives and official guides who are supposed to know every inch of the city, however, knew nothing of this discovery. I pressed him with questions which he tried to evade, but could not. Finally after the pictures were taken, I complimented him on the marvelous discovery of the tomb of St. Peter that the Franciscans had made. He was clearly nervous as he said, "Oh, no. The tomb of St. Peter is in Rome." But as he said that, his voice faltered, a fact which even my friend, Mr. Mattar, noticed. Then I looked him squarely in the eyes and said, "No. The tomb of St. Peter is in Jerusalem." He looked at me like a guilty school boy and said nothing. He was, no doubt, placed there to hide facts, but his actions and words, to anyone who knows anything about human nature, spoke more eloquently than those priests who whole-heartedly admitted the truth.

I also spoke to a Franciscan priest in authority in

the priest's printing plant within the walls of old Jerusalem, where the book on the subject was printed. He also admitted that the tomb of St. Peter is in Jerusalem. Then, when I was visiting the Church of the Nativity in Bethlehem, I encountered a Franciscan monk. After declaring to him what a wonderful discovery the Franciscans had made, the discovery of the tomb of St. Peter, I asked him plainly, "Do you folks really believe that those are the bones of St. Peter?"

He responded, "Yes, we do. We have no choice in the matter. The clear evidence is there."

Then I asked, "So Father Bagatti (co-writer of the book on the subject, and archeologist) really believes that those are the bones of St. Peter?"

"Yes, he does," he responded.

Then I asked, "But what does the Pope think of all this?"

"Well," he answered, "Father Bagatti told me personally that three years ago he went to the Pope in Rome and showed him the evidence, and the Pope said to him, Well, we will have to make some changes, but for the time being, let us keep this thing quiet.' "

Then I said, "So the Pope (Pius XII) really believed that those were the bones of St. Peter?"

"Yes," was his answer, "The documentary evidence is there; he could not help believing."

I visited various renowned archeologists on the subject. Dr. Albright of John Hopkins University in Baltimore told me that he personally knew Priest Bagatti and that he was a very competent archeologist. I also spoke with Dr. Nelson Glueck, archeologist and president of the Hebrew Union College in Cincinnati. I showed him the pictures found in this booklet, and he quickly recognized the Aramaic words to be "Simon Bar Jona" (Armaic is very similar to Hebrew).

I asked him whether he would write a statement to that effect. He said to do so would cast a reflection on the competency of the Priest J. T. Milik, whom he knew to be a very able scientist. But he said that he would write a note to that effect. I quote, "I regard Father J. T. Milik as a first-class scholar in the Semitic field." He added, "I do not consider that names on ossuaries (bone-boxes) are conclusive evidence that they are those of the Apostles.

Nelson Glueck"

Naturally, Dr. Glueck is right, for the only positive proof a person could have would be to witness Peter's death and to be at his burial and then eight to ten years later when the body had decomposed, to watch men uncover the grave and place the bones in an ossuary, marked with Peter's name, as was the Roman custom in those days. Of course, such certainty is out of the question; and even if there was a record of such a witness, it still would not be absolute proof to anyone other than the witness. The report would be accepted as proof, if it were established in the Bible or history, but such is not the case. But for all practical purposes and to honest open minds, there can be no doubt in the matter.

As I mentioned, I had a very agreeable talk with Priest Milik, but I did not have the opportunity to see Priest Bagatti while I was in Jerusalem. I wrote to him however, on March 15, 1960. I wrote as follows: "I have spoken with a number of Franciscan priests and monks, and they have told me about you and the book of which you are co-writer. I had hoped to meet you and to compliment you on such a great discovery, but time would not permit. Having heard so much about you and that you are an archeologist [and with

15

the evidence in hand], I was very much convinced, with you, concerning the ancient Christian burial ground that the remains found in the bone-box with the name on it, Simon Bar Jona, written in Aramaic, were those of St. Peter." It is remarkable that in his reply he did not contradict my statement, "I was very much convinced with you . . . that the remains found in the bone-box . . . were those of St. Peter." This confirms the talk I had with the Franciscan monk in Bethlehem and the story he told me of Priest Bagatti's going to the Pope with the evidence concerning the bones of St. Peter in Jerusalem. In his letter one can see that he is careful because of the Pope's admonition to keep this discovery quiet. He therefore wrote me that he leaves the whole explanation of the Aramaic words, "Simon Bar Jona," to Priest Milik. In the book written by the two men in 1958, Milik makes some suggestions that the inscriptions could refer to a person of a similar name. In the end, however, he admits that the early interpretation (of Priest Bagatti) could be true. Priest Bagatti had made a clear statement in his article ("Scoperta di um cimitero giudo-cristiano: . . . Apina Aedem Flagetationi," 1953, pp. 149-184) that the Aramaic writing on the box, "Simon Bar Jona," was clearly and beautifully written. But after seeing the Pope and being instructed to keep the matter quiet, he leaves the judgment of the matter with his co-writer, Milik. In Bagatti's letter one can see that he is in a difficult position. He cannot go against what he had written in 1953, at the time of the discovery of this Christian-Jewish burial ground, nor what he had said to the Franciscan monk about his visit to the Pope, but he does raise a question. He writes, "Supposing that it is 'Jona' (on the bone box), as I believe, it may be some other relative of St. Peter, because names were passed on from family to family. To be able to propose the identification of it with St. Peter would go against a long tradition, which has its own value. Anyway another volume will come soon that will demonstrate that the cemetery was Christian and of the 1-11 century A.D.

The salute in God

most devoted

P. B. Bagatti

O. F. M."

As I said before, it is most remarkable, that, though he insinuated a question which could lead one from the truth, he did not contradict me. He certainly would have denied his belief, if he conscientiously could have done so — when I clearly wrote, "I was very much convinced with you . . . that the remains found in the bone-box with the name on it in Aramaic, 'Simon Bar Jona,' were those of St. Peter."

To Protestants, it matters little where Peter's body was buried, since they know he himself is in Heaven. But for the adherents of the Catholic Church to build their superstructure on Peter and to claim that he was their first Pope in Rome and that he was martyred and buried there, is a very unstable foundation. The Bible says in 1 Cor. 3:11, "Other foundation can no man lay than that is laid, which is Jesus Christ." Also it is written, "Cursed be man that trusteth in man." I am reminded of a story which an ex-priest told me in Scotland two months ago. A discussion over religion with a Protestant caused him to study the Bible and to think seriously about his beliefs. Finally he found salvation through Christ and then left the priesthood. The Protestant told him that his religion had saved

Peter from drowning. The priest questioned, "What do you mean by saying that your religion saved Peter from drowning?"

"Well," responded the Protestant, "one day when Peter was walking on the water, he began to sink. Then he called upon Jesus with all his heart, and He saved him." Even Mary exclaimed, in Luke 1:47, "My spirit hath rejoiced in God my Savior." If Peter and Mary could do nothing to save themselves and they needed a Savior, how much more can they not save us? It is written, "Whosoever shall call on the name of the Lord shall be saved." Again the Bible says, "Believe on the Lord Jesus Christ and thou shalt be saved." Just try calling only on the Lord Jesus Christ with all your heart, asking Him to forgive your sins and to come into your heart and life, and see what happens.

This ancient Christian burial ground shows that Peter died and was buried in Jerusalem, which is easily understandable since neither history or the Bible tells of Peter being in Rome. To make matters more clear, the Bible tells us that Peter was the Apostle to the Jews. It was Paul who was called the Apostle to the Gentiles, and both history and the Bible tell of his being in Rome. No wonder that the Roman Catholic Bishop Strossmayer in his great speech (as given in my book, The Rise and Fall of the Roman Catholic Church) against Papal Infallibility, before the Pope and the Council of 1870, said, "Scaliger, one of the most learned of men, has not hesitated to say that St. Peter's episcopate and residence at Rome ought to be classed with ridiculous legends."

The secrecy surrounding this case is amazing, and yet understandable, since the Catholics largely base their faith on the assumption that Peter was their first Pope in Rome and that he was martyred and buried there. But I am somewhat of the opinion that the Franciscan priests, who are honest, would be glad to see the truth go out, even if it displeases those who are over them. While visiting with Priest Milik, I told him of the highly educated priest with whom I had spoken just before going from Rome to Jerusalem. He admitted to me that the remains of Peter are not in the tomb of St. Peter's in Rome. I asked him what had happened to them? He responded, "We don't know, but we think that the Saracens stole them away." First of all, the Saracens never got to Rome, but even if they had, what would they want with the bones of Peter? We had a good laugh over that, but we really laughed together when I told him of my discussion with a brilliant American priest in Rome. I asked this American priest if he knew that the bones of Peter were not in the tomb of St. Peter in Rome. He admitted that they were not there. However, he said that a good friend of his, an archeologist, had been excavating under St. Peter's for the bones of St. Peter for a number of years, and five years ago he found them. Now a man can be identified by his finger prints, but never by his bones. So I asked him how he knew they were the bones of St. Peter. He responded that they had taken the bones to a chemist, and they were analyzed, and it was judged that the bones were of a man who had died about the age of 65 years; therefore, they must be Peter's. Mark you, all the priests agree that the Vatican and St. Peter's were built over a pagan cemetery, a very appropriate place for them to build. You realize, surely, that Pagans would never bury a Christian in their own burial ground, and you may be very sure that the Christians would never bury their dead in a Pagan cemetery. So, even if Peter died in Rome, which is even foolish to suppose, surely the pagan cemetery under St. Peter's would be the last place he would have been buried.

After returning from Jerusalem to Rome, I talked to a number of other priests over the subject, and it was then that I arrived at the conclusion that there are almost as many "traditional" theories concerning the tomb of St. Peter in Rome as there are priests in Rome, and each theory seems more ridiculous than the others, if one takes the time to think over them and to investigate them. One priest admitted that the bones of Peter are not nor ever have been in the tomb of St. Peter in Rome, but they must be somewhere in Rome, "for the skulls of Peter and Paul are in the Church of St. John in the Lateran." It was a queer story, but I went to that church to check. Yes, the official caretaker assured me that the skulls of Peter and Paul were there, but he did not know where. It was clear that he wanted to change the subject. I did learn, however, that the same church had over 660 pounds of gold as ornament on the walls, but worse yet, the nearby church, Sta. Maria Maggori, the keeper told me, has 1520 pounds of gold on its walls, a total of the two churches being worth well over a million dollars. Lloyd's of London, one of their depositories of money, some years ago served notice on the Vatican that they would have to circulate their vast amount of money, as it could not remain there idle. When they give anything to the poor (a marvelous sales talk for raising money), they have the poor make a long waiting line outside the church in the heat, rain, or cold, to parade to the world that they are giving to the poor. But if you would examine what was given, you would say that it was hardly worth while taking home. Judging from appearances, if five cents out of every dollar they collect for charity, goes for charity it is a lot. Many times I have heard from Catholics themselves, of cases in South America where sobbing mothers have brought their sickly newborn babies to the priest for baptism before they died, but were refused, because the parent had no money to pay the price of baptism. It is hard to imagine anything more horrible, since they really believe that the child without baptism may any moment slip into hell. To make matters worse, the heartless creature stands there refusing baptism until payment is made. Not all are like that, but you can count the vast majority among them. Now to get back to the skulls. After I left the church, the supposed resting place of the skulls, I went to the nearby Franciscan quarters, and there met the priest who had sold me the book some months before, and he told me that he had never heard that the skulls of Peter and Paul were ever found, and in other words, he told me that my newly found "skull" information was "rubbish," to which I agreed. "To be sure," he said, "the official guide book tells nothing of such." For my benefit he went through his guide book, and soon declared that the story was given as a legend, which he stated was ridiculous. Not even their almost "infallible" tradition is certain on the subject, judging from the many stories which pass as "tradition" that you hear from the priests.

The Pope was right, going back to the early Christian burial ground, they must make changes, and many of them and fundamental ones at that. But I am afraid that the Pope's remark was made to satisfy Priest Bagatti, by admitting the truth, but admonishing him to keep the information quiet, hoping that the information would die out. But now they are saying that after all these years of excavation, since 1939, they have discovered Greek words which read, "Peter is

21

buried here," and it gives the date as 160 A.D. First of all, the very structure of the sentence immediately gives one the impression that either quite recently or long ago, someone put that sign there, hoping that it would be taken as authentic in order to establish that which then, and even now, has never been proven. Then there is a discrepancy in the date, for Peter was martyred around the year 67, and not 160 A.D. Thirdly, why is it that they mention nothing about finding bones under or around the sign? While visiting the Catacombs, one sees a few things which are not becoming to Christians, but which tend to indicate that the Christians had some pagan practices, similar to those of Rome today. Nothing is said about them and only after persistent questioning, will the Roman Catholic priest, who acts as guide, tell you that those things were placed there centuries after the early Christian era.

What does all this mean? It means that everything connected with Catholicism is a part of the whole. Jesus said, "A corrupt tree bringeth forth corrupt fruit," as we see in the following: The corruption which comes through the celibacy of the priests and nuns; the unnatural hiding away from the world in Convents and Monasteries; the inhuman, un-American, and un-Scriptural prohibition of their people to read and examine both sides of questions other than those the hierarchy allows; in other words, the enslavement of the intellect and the soul through fear; the unreasonable and un-Scriptural doctrine of Purgatory, images and prayers to the Saints, which are absolutely foreign to the Bible. Even Jerome, who translated the Bible which was used in the Catholic Church for a thousand years, said that the Apocryphal books, where only slight mention of some of the above are found, are

22

false, being apocryphal; the doctrine of salvation by works rather than through faith in Christ, who alone can transform the lives of men. Good works can never transform a person, but a simple, complete and whole-hearted trust and surrender to Christ can. Good works are prompted by salvation, but good works can never bring about salvation; the erroneous principle of building their church upon man, rather than the Son of God.

It is very doubtful whether Pope John XXIII will make the many necessary revolutionary changes throughout the Roman Catholic system. It will be interesting, moreover, to see whether he will acknowledge the great discovery of the tomb of St. Peter in Jerusalem. If he does not admit the validity of the discovery, will he be silent, or will he try to overthrow the weight of truth?

CHAPTER TWO

If Peter Was Pope

If Peter was Pope, it was the unescapable duty of Paul and the other Apostles to acknowledge him as such, but nowhere in the Bible do we find anything of the sort. The Apostle Paul, in opening his letter to the Romans, does not write to "his excellent highness, Pope Peter," no, he writes in Romans 1:7: "To all that be in Rome, beloved of God." Peter refers to Paul as brother Paul, which clearly shows that Peter was anything but Pope, in fact, he writes in his own epistle, I Peter 5:1: "The elders which are among you I exhort, who am also an elder." This statement makes you feel closer to Peter. It is just as Christ said to His disciples in John 15:15: "Henceforth I call you not servants, for the servant knoweth not what his lord doeth: but I have called you friends."

If Peter was Pope, he would never have ruled over temporal powers, as popes do, for he knew that Jesus had said, "My kingdom is not of this world" (John 18:36). And Jesus, also said, "Render unto Caesar the things that are Caesar's; and unto God the things that are God's" (Matt. 22:21). Also, "Neither be ye called masters, for one is your Master, even Christ" (Matt. 23:10).

If Peter was Pope (or not), he would never have made tradition equal with the Word of God, for he

24

knew the Scripture, "Beware lest any man spoil you through philosophy and vain deceit, after the *traditions* of men, after the rudiments of the world, and not after Christ . . . and ye are complete in Him" (Col. 2:8-10). Also he knew the words of Christ in Mark 7:9-13: "Full well ye reject the commandments of God, that ye may keep your own *tradition* . . . making the word of God of none effect through your *tradition.*" Peter, himself, wrote in 1 Peter 1:18: "Forasmuch as ye know that ye were not redeemed with corruptible things, as silver and gold, from your vain conversation received by *tradition* from your fathers." Even Jerome said, "As we accept those things that are written [in the Bible], so we reject those things that are not written [in the Bible]." It is interesting that not only are the traditions of Rome not in the Bible, but they are against the Bible, and against the early fathers of the Church, naturally.

If Peter was Pope, he would have written much if not all of his work from Rome — but not a word from Peter from Rome. He never acted like a Pope. He was humble as were the rest of the Apostles. It has never been recorded that anyone ever kissed his feet When Cornelius met Peter, the Bible says (Acts 10:25-26): "Cornelius fell down and worshipped him. But Peter took him up, saying, Stand up; I myself also am a man." To be sure, nobody ever kissed his ring, for he did not have a ring. He said, "Silver and gold have I none."

Jesus said in Matt. 9:6: "That ye may know that the Son of Man hath power on earth to forgive sins (then saith he to the sick of the palsy), Arise, take up thy bed, and go unto thine house. And he arose, and departed to his house." Jesus said: "Whether it is easier to say, Thy sins be forgiven thee; or to say,

25

Arise and walk?" If the Pope and the priests do not have power to say, "Arise, take up thy bed and walk," surely they do not have power to forgive sins either. Peter never said to anyone, "Thy sins be forgiven thee," but under the power of the Holy Ghost, Peter in Acts 3:6, said to the cripple, "Silver and gold have I none; but such as I have give I thee. In the name of Jesus Christ of Nazareth rise up and walk." Jesus in Matt. 18:18, was talking to his disciples, and of course the Apostles as well, when He said, "Whatsoever ye shall bind on earth shall be bound in heaven: and whatsoever ye shall loose on earth shall be loosed in heaven." Jesus had just prior to this told them how they should treat an offending brother, and if finally he would listen to reason, they would win their brother, but if not, after following the Lord's instruction, to account him "as a heathen man." I worked 14 years in a factory and part of that time as a paint tinter, together with an Irish Catholic. He did everything he could to ruin me in the eyes of our employer. I would be working with one hundred gallons of paint at a time, and he would do all he could to cause something to happen to ruin the paint while it was under my care. I would not fight with him, but with this verse in mind (about loosing and binding) I would call on the Lord to look down and to undertake. It was almost laughable how his tricks fell to his own hurt, and finally he had to quit the work.

Peter used the same power against Ananias and Sapphira, who dropped dead. Paul used the same power against Elymas the sorcerer, who was blinded. But never did the Apostles or Christians, or even the early fathers of the Church, ever say, "Thy sins be forgiven thee," for as the Scriptures record, "Who can forgive sins but God only?" (Mark 2:7). There is another

26

Scripture the priests use to try to prove that people ought to confess to them, but again the very Scripture they use is proof against them. The Scripture is found in James 5:16, "Confess your faults one to another." From this by no stretch of the imagination could one gather that one must confess one's faults to the priest, and he to the bishop, and the bishop to the arch-bishop, etc. It is clearly stated here, that — well, there is no clearer way of explaining it than as it is written: "One to another," and not, "One to the other." If we admit our faults "One to another" we are on the same common ground, otherwise one lords it over the other. You will notice it says nothing about forgiving other's sins, only in that they have offended us. When we forgive our brother God forgives, and when we do all in our power to win our brother, but he does not admit his fault to us, then his sin is held or bound in heaven. To say that any man can forgive sins committed against another person or against God is the basest type of perversion.

A young woman, some years ago, was converted from a life of sin. One night two of her former associates followed her as she was going home through a park after attending an evening Gospel meeting. They were determined to force her to go with them and drag her back into sin. She was a new convert, but she turned on them, and in the power of the Holy Spirit, she said, "I rebuke you in the name of Jesus." One of the gangsters dropped dead on the spot and the other ran for his life. When in court she was asked by the police to repeat the words that she said to the gangsters, and when the police saw the power of God come upon her as she was about to repeat those words again, they all cried out, "Never mind, you don't have to repeat them!" They were afraid the curse might fall upon them as well.

If Peter was Pope, he would have excommunicated the Apostle Paul and all the other Apostles, and had them burned at the stake as schismatics and heretics, for Paul severely reprimanded Peter, saying, in Gal. 2:11: "When Peter was come to Antioch, I withstood him to the face, because he was to be blamed." All the Apostles with one accord told Peter to go to Samaria, we read in Acts 8:14: "When the Apostles which were at Jerusalem heard that Samaria had received the word of God, they sent unto them Peter and John." This act of the Apostles was a sacrilege and a scandal — if Peter was Pope. Paul takes authority over the Church of Rome, as he writes in Romans 16:17: "Now I beseech you, brethren, mark them which cause divisions and offences contrary to the doctrine which ye have learned, and avoid them." In the 15th chapter of Acts, we read of the 1st Council at Jerusalem. The story was this, that in Antioch some had taught a false doctrine, and Paul and Barnabas, who were there preaching at the time, disputed against these false teachings. And as it is written, "they (the ordinary Christians) determined that Paul and Barnabas, and certain of them, should go up to Jerusalem unto *the apostles and elders* about the question." Notice here, if all Popes were infallible in doctrine, as they say — surely Peter would have had the highest and purest type of infallibility in matters of doctrine, and no one from the most ignorant to the most intelligent in the church would have failed to recognize it. But here it tells us (and you find the same incident in the same place in the Catholic Bible) that the Christians in Antioch "determined that Paul and Barnabas, and certain of them, should go up to Jerusalem unto the *apostles and elders* about this question." They were not going to consult with Peter, "the infallible Pope," but with the "apostles and elders." Paul and Barnabas spoke, so did Peter, but it was James who passed the sentence which was accepted by all. By this incident alone, only an insane person could fail to see that Peter was not a Pope, and also that he was not infallible in doctrine, or they would have gone only to Peter. To prove further the point, the Apostles wrote, in verse 28, "For is seemed good to the Holy Ghost, and to us," showing they all agreed with the sentence which was of James and not of Peter. Paul wrote that he was nothing behind the very chiefest Apostles" (2 Cor. 12:11). For the cause of Christ, Paul traveled more, suffered more and wrote more than all the other Apostles.

Peter could never be Pope for he was a married man, as we see in Mark 1:30-31: "Simon's wife's mother lay sick of a fever, and anon they tell him of her. And he came and took her by the hand, and lifted her up; and immediately the fever left her, and she ministered unto them." "St. Petronilla was the daughter of Peter. Her chapel founded by the French Government may be seen in the Basilica of St. Peter at the Vatican in Rome." Paul also shows that Peter was with his wife long after Christ arose from the grave. Paul writes in 1 Cor. 9:5: "Have we not the power to lead about a sister, a wife, as well as other apostles, and as the brethren of the Lord, and Cephas (Peter)?" One that is single can never penetrate into the understanding and unity that comes to married couples' lives. Likewise, childless married couples can never know the feeling and the close attachment that comes to those who have children. A bachelor can never understand home life and the intricacies associated, yet thousands of bachelor Roman Catholic priests try to tell families what to

29

do. Apostle Paul wrote in 1 Tim. 3:2-5: "A bishop then must be blameless, the husband of one wife . . . one that ruleth well his own house, having his children in subjection with all gravity; for if a man know not how to rule his own house, how shall he take care of the Church of God?" That the priests do not marry, I believe, is one of the reasons why the Romish Church has apostatised from the Bible.

Pope Gregory VII declared all clerical marriages invalid. "Our judgment upon marriages contracted by persons of this kind (the clergy) is that they must be broken." (First Lateran Council 1123, Canon XXI). Peter was "an example to the flock"; he would never have divorced his wife for he knew that there was only one Biblical reason for leaving or divorcing one's wife, and that was infidelity. The above declaration proves that the clergy were in the custom of being married up until the year of 1123 A.D., or else he would not have declared "must be broken." The priests all say, when you tell them of all their new inventions, that these are not new inventions, they were always there, but it is only that they are from time to time officially recognized. But this declaration has them up a tree. It also proves that the Popes are not infallible, in doctrine or morals, for the Popes before Pope Gregory VII (1123) accepted priests who were married and allowed those who were not to get married, for they were the only ones who gave licences, especially to their own clergy.

If Peter was Pope, he would never have accepted the title "Vicar of Christ," and certainly Christ never gave it to him or anyone else. Peter knew the Scripture that says in Eph. 5:23, "Christ is the head of the Church," and this was written after Christ had ascended into heaven. So Christ never relinquished His position as head of the Church. Peter also knew the words of Christ in John 14:26: "The comforter, which is the Holy Ghost, whom the Father will send in my name, he shall teach you all things, and bring all things to your remembrance, whatsoever I have said unto you." Also Peter knew that Jesus said: "When he, the Spirit of truth, is come, he will guide you into all truth." There was no need then, or is there now, for a religious dictator or Pope. In fact, according to the Scriptures above, a Pope is a usurper. Thank God the Evangelicals never had one and I trust never will. Peter wrote of Jesus, "Ye were as sheep going astray; but are now returned unto the Shepherd and Bishop of your souls" (1 Peter 2:25).

Peter never assumed the position of Pope and nowhere in the Bible does it show in all the relations between the Apostles, disciples, Christians and Christ where anyone acknowledged him as such. What a funny Pope! Never acted like a Pope, never dressed like a Pope, never spoke like a Pope, never wrote like a Pope, and no one ever approached him as though he were a Pope. Why is that? The answer is very simple. He never was a Pope. To call Peter, much less those who call themselves successors of Peter, "King of kings and Lord of lords" is nothing short of blasphemy, for that title belongs only to Christ. The reason Peter did not assume the title of Pope, and the reason the Apostles did not consider him as such, was because they knew exactly what Jesus meant when He said in Matt. 16:19: "Thou are Peter (Petrus), and upon this rock (Petram) I will build my church; and the gates of hell shall not prevail against it." In the Latin there are two different words "Petrus" for Peter and "Petram" for "Rock." In Greek it is equally clear. It is "Petros" for Peter and "Petra" for "Rock." Christ was a master of languages, and if the Roman Catholic

31

system, that hangs its very existence on the above Scripture, was of God, surely He would have said, as any child would have, "Thou art Peter and upon *you* will I build my Church." Peter and the Apostles knew better, as also did the early fathers of the Church. Clement, Polycarp, Ireneus, Tertullian, Jerome and Augustine, who were for the most part disciples of the Apostles, would surely have known the certainty of the matter of Popery, and it would have been an impossibility for them not to mention Popery and the "Extremely Holy" fisherman. Such language, to one who reads the Bible, is ridiculous. One reads statements from Peter and the Apostles directed to Christians in general, calling them "Fellow heirs," "brethren," and "sojourners together." St. Augustine and Jerome, as well as other early fathers, believed as in the words of Augustine, "He did not say to him, 'Thou art Petra,' but 'Thou art Petros,' for Christ is Petra." In Eph. 2:20 we read: "Jesus Christ himself being the chief corner stone."

As for apostolic succession, Peter knew that was all rubbish, for he it was who originated the idea which did not work out. The Catholics founded their Church on Peter and, as we shall see, on his mistakes. Peter learned by his mistakes, but the Catholic Church does not learn by Peter's or their own. In Acts 1:20, Peter quotes a prophecy in Psalms, saying, "For it is written in the book of Psalms, Let his (Judas') habitation be desolate, and let no man dwell therein: and his bishoprick let another take." Peter was right that another should take the place of Judas, but he did not know that the Lord had other plans. Peter was one of them who suggested in the 23rd verse the appointment of two men and that lots should be drawn between them. The lot fell on Matthias — but you never hear of him again.

But the Lord had a wonderful way of bringing Paul on the scene and He Himself placing Paul in the place of "chiefest of Apostles." We read in 1 Cor. 12:28 of the place Jesus has in His Church and has never given to another: "God hath set some in the church, first Apostles, secondly prophets, thirdly teachers." Apostolic succession is a farce, we see by this Scripture, for it is God and not man who chooses His servants. Much less can they do so who so thoroughly reject the word of God. But the Catholic Church faithfully follows the errors of Peter. Peter resorted to the sword; so do they. Peter preached false doctrines (as we see elsewhere in this book); so do they. Peter denied Christ; so do they by usurping Christ's authority, saying that the Pope takes Christ's place on earth. Nobody can take Christ's place on earth. Such an attitude is blasphemous, for He never relinquished His place over the Church. Peter rebuked Christ when Christ told the disciples that He must "suffer many things of the elders, and chief priests and scribes, and be killed, and be raised again on the third day. "Then Peter took Him, and began to rebuke Him, saying: be it far from thee, Lord; this shall not be done unto thee." This is the spirit of presumption, "which opposeth and exalteth itself above all that is called God, or that is worshipped." In the chapter called "Ruy Barbosa Speaks," (in the book, "The Rise and Fall of the Roman Catholic Church") you will read their own words showing how they exalt themselves above God. The fact, as well, is revealed that they put their "traditions" on equality with and superceding the Bible, the Word of God. That Peter rebuked Jesus shows that he desired the pre-eminence (for there had been strife amongst the apostles as to who should be the greatest), which the Roman Catholic seeks to this very day. But Christ

33

rebuked Peter in these words, as in Matt. 16:23: Jesus "turned and said unto Peter, Get thee behind me, Satan; thou savourest not the things that be of God, but those that be of men." Peter learned by his mistakes, but Popery continues in Peter's mistakes. They say their Church was founded on Peter. It is a more than evident fact. The Christian Churches are founded on the solid Rock, Christ Jesus.

Whenever questions arise about the Bible, you can always look to the Bible for the answer. Let us turn to Eph. 2:19-20: "Ye [all "born-again" Christians] are built upon the foundation of the *Apostles* and *prophets, Jesus Christ himself being the chief corner stone;* in whom all the building fitly framed together groweth unto an holy temple in the Lord." Thank God, this is the Spiritual Church, which the gates of Hell shall not prevail against, and those whose sins are forgiven and washed away by the blood of the Lamb of God are a part thereof. It is true, "For other foundation can no man lay than that which is laid, which is Jesus Christ." 1 Cor. 3:11.

If Peter was Pope, he would never have written, in 1 Peter 2:13: "Submit yourselves to every ordinance of man for the Lord's sake; whether it be to the king, as supreme, or unto governors." For according to the contrary view, "The Pope has the right to pronounce sentence of deposition against any sovereign, when required by the good of the [his] spiritual order." (Brownson's Review, Vol. 1. page 48). Neither Christ nor Peter nor the Apostles or ministers of the Gospel of all time ever took this un-Christian stand, as seen in their statement which is in contradiction to the verse of Scripture written by Peter.

If Peter was Pope, Christ would never have said as written in Matt. 5:44: "Love your enemies, bless them that curse you, do good to them that hate you, and pray for them which despitefully use you and persecute you." In all Catholic countries today the Protestants are persecuted in a manner that is not human, to say nothing of being uncivilized and un-Christian, as they have done in all ages. There is a great conspiracy going on against the Protestant nations, and they are using the "spider-and-fly" confidence method as a means, and outright misrepresentations as another means. Dictators recognized the value of the approach the present Pope is adopting. To visit the hospitals, and jails, and give flowers to the sick, and fondle little children, patting them on the cheeks before a few dozen photographers makes marvelous propaganda. Another method is their clever way of making the people think that the Catholic Church is not what it used to be. But their statements found in this book, which were not meant for the general public, and which were never taken back, will show you that, as they themselves say, "Rome never changes." If they had changed they would admit their guilt in the terrible Inquisition, and the murder of the Huguenots, and in the Second World War, and the outrages going on in Catholic countries today. The following statements have never been revoked, therefore you can be sure they represent the real Romish Church behind its mask.

"Father Hecker declares that ' 'ere long there is to be a state religion in the country [U. S. A.], and that state religion is to be Roman Catholic.' Bishop O'Conner, of Pittsburgh, says: Religious liberty is merely endured until the opposite can be carried into effect, without peril to the Catholic world.' The Archbishop of St. Louis declares: 'If Catholics ever, which they surely will, gain an immense numerical majority,

religious freedom in this country will be at an end.' "
"Rome in America," by Justin D. Fulton, D.D.

Then we read: "Liberty is today's major plague," Hunter Guthrie, S. J., head of the Jesuit University. Also we read: "No one doubts that they (apostates) do not merely deserve to be cut off from the Church by excommunication but that they deserve to be put to death . . . so as soon as any man publicly professes heresy and tries by word or example to pervert others . . . he may justly be put to death." (From a manual of Canon Law, by Fr. (later cardinal) Lepicier of the Roman University. This manual was officially endorsed by Pius X (quoted in the Convert, October, 1957). Nice people, these Popes.

If Peter was Pope he would never have written in Acts 4:12: "Neither is there Salvation in any other: for there is none other name under heaven given among men, whereby we must be saved." Nor would Christ have said, in John 3:16: "For God so loved the world, that he gave his only begotten Son, that *whosoever believeth in him* should not perish, but have everlasting life." Also in Romans 8:14: "For as many as are led by the *Spirit of God* (not the Pope), they are the sons of God." The Catholic teaching has always been and is today, in spite of clever Catholic propaganda to the contrary, as Cardinal Marchetti Selvaggianni writes: "Among those things which the Church has always preached and will never cease to preach is contained also that infallible statement by which we are taught that there is no salvation outside the Church." (From a letter addressed to Archbishop Cushing of Boston by the Sacred Congregation of the Holy Office. Quoted in the "Catholic Mind," December, 1952.)

If Peter was Pope he would never call himself infallible, as the Pope called himself in 1870, and thereby calling all others before and since then — and to be sure, their "1st Pope Peter." St. Peter, and everybody else, knew how many mistakes he made before Christ was crucified and after. He denied Christ and was accused by Apostle Paul of false teaching. Peter knew that to be infallible, or to be the "Vicar of Christ," one would have to be infallible in everything, as Christ and the Holy Spirit are infallible. Peter knew that and so did the Popes, but the Popes shrewdly narrowed the word down to "Doctrine and morals." If they could have concealed the extreme corruption in the lives of many of their Popes they would have held their Popes up to be infallible in all things, as the title "Vicar of Christ" would demand. But even though they apply the infallibility of the Popes only to "Doctrine and morals" (by all means they should drop morals), even in their teaching they clearly contradict the Bible as Popes have contradicted other Popes, who have gone on to "Purgatory." Oh, yes! they order masses to be said all over the world for Popes when they die. You would think that if he has the keys of Heaven and Hell he would surely use one of them to get himself into Heaven. If he cannot use them in his own behalf, surely he cannot use them in favour or against anybody else. Too, with a little reflection, if the Pope, for instance, is so infallible in teaching and morals, why does he not have, after nearly 1,600 years, a little consideration for his subjects and use just a little of his infallibility, together with some concentration, and let the people clearly know whether the suffering in Purgatory is "pleasantly endured" as some Catholic authorities say (if it were true it would save people billions yearly; for why worry if it isn't bad?), or whether they suffer up to "millions of centuries" (as others say), the sufferings which are much more terrible than though they were by fire? If the Pope would read his Bible he would know that there is no such place as a "good" or "bad" Purgatory. We read in 1 John 1:7: "The blood of Jesus Christ his Son cleanseth us from all sin." But since he does not want to follow the Bible, he should at least make up his mind as to which of the two schools of thought in Catholicism is right. However, on second thought, knowing Popes as you do, you could hardly expect them to be too clear on the subject; for whereas they could save their subjects billions of dollars annually, it would be to their own loss. Just think what you could do with a billion or two annually.

If Peter was Pope, I suppose he would have felt at home, in a way, in a chair, carried on the shoulders of men. The up and down motion would remind him of his fishing days at sea. However, if he were dressed in the humble clothes of a fisherman, or apostle, he would be a comical sight to a crowd who were used to great pomp, ceremony, show and make believe. On the other hand, if he were dressed in the gaudy splendour of the Popes, I am sure he would feel as out of place as David, the shepherd boy, felt in the heavy armour of the giant, Saul. The whole affair is enough to make Peter turn over in his grave, but they are not afraid of that, for they say they have the head of Peter, in gold, in one place and Peter's bones are supposed to be buried in another place. This is a perfect example as to what extent they will go to hold their people in darkness and superstition.

Peter would never have been Pope, for he was an "ensample to the flock." Popery says, "don't do as I do but do as I say." These two statements are contradictory. Peter was like Paul, who said, contrary to the Papists, "Follow me as I follow Christ." The difference is great. Besides the hypocrisy of the priests who do not practice what they preach, one follows the priests, or else follows Christ. You cannot serve two masters.

The word Pope was not in use until the wicked emperor Phocas gave it to the Bishop of Rome in 610. This the emperor did to spite the Bishop Circiacus of Constantinople, who had justly excommunicated him for his having caused the assassination of his predecessor, Emperor Mauritius, Gregory I, then Bishop of Rome, refused the title of Pope, but his successor, Boniface III, was the first to assume the title of Pope in 610 A.D. (J.D. Lewen.)

Romish leaders are free moral agents, and they can steer their Church as they please — and it seems that is exactly what they are doing. But is it possible that they never read their Bibles? Paul in Romans 11: 13 writes, "I am the apostle of the Gentiles" (to us, who are not Hebrews). In Galatians, Paul says, "The Gospel of the circumcision (unto the Jews) was unto Peter." Then the Apostle Paul writes in 2 Cor. 11:28, "That which cometh upon me daily, the care of all the churches." Does all this look as though Peter was the Pope of the Gentiles and head of the Church? The Apostle Paul would have been a more likely candidate for such an unscriptural post.

If Peter was Pope, and the rock upon which the Church was to be founded, the Scripture in 1 Cor. 3:11, would never have been written: "For other foundation can no man lay than that is laid, which is Jesus Christ." Also Jesus would never have said, in Mark 10:44: "Whosoever of you will be chiefest shall be servant of all." Then, too, Peter would never have allowed pagan doctrines and practices to enter the Church—and you may be sure they did not while the Apostles were alive.

Cardinal Newman, in his book, "The Development

of the Christian Religion," page 359, admits that "Temples, incense, oil lamps, votive offerings, holy water, holidays and seasons of devotion, processions, blessing of fields, sacerdotal vestments, the tonsure (of priests, monks and nuns), images . . . are of pagan origin." It is interesting to note the following, as seen by one who was there, "nowhere in these strange burial places (Catacombs) did these early Christians inscribe on the walls any thought of prayer for the dead, nor did they dream of the Cross or Crucifix as a Christian symbol." ("A Protestant Pilgrimage to Rome," by J. A. Kensit.)

If Peter was Pope in Rome, it would have been Peter and not Paul who would have written to the churches. Peter wrote altogether only eight chapters, but Paul wrote 100 chapters. Yes, it would have been Peter's place to have written to the churches in various countries. But not a letter, not a sentence, not a word, not a sermon, not even one admonition came from Peter from Rome. It is strange, is it not, and yet they say Peter was Pope in Rome from the year 41 to 66 A.D., a period of 25 years. But let us see where Peter was during these years.

The book of the Acts of the Apostles (in either the Catholic or the Protestant Bible) records the following. Peter was preaching the Gospel to the circumcision (the Jews) in Caesaria and Joppa in Palestine, ministering unto the household of Cornelius, which is a distance of 1,800 miles from Rome (Acts 10:23, 24). About the year 44 A.D. (Acts 12:9) Peter was cast into prison in Jerusalem by Herod, but he was released by an angel. From 46 to 52 A.D., we read in the 15th Chapter that he was in Jerusalem preaching the difference between Law and Grace. Saul was converted in 34 A.D. and became Paul the Apostle (Acts 9). Paul tells us that three years after his conversion in 37 A.D. he "went up to Jerusalem to see Peter" (Gal. 1:18), and in 51 A.D. — fourteen years later — he again went up to Jerusalem (Gal. 2:1), Peter being mentioned. Soon after this he met Peter in Antioch, and as Paul says rebuked Peter "to the face," because he was to be blamed (Gal. 2:11). Paul makes a wonderful statement which casts a great deal of light on the subject. Paul writes, "I am ready to preach the Gospel to you that are at Rome also" (Rom. 1:15). Then in Rom. 15:20: "For so have I strived to preach the Gospel, not where *Christ was named*, lest I should build on another man's foundation." These words make things very clear. Certainly if Peter had been in Rome between the years 41 and 66 A.D. he would have preached Christ and Paul then could not have, in the year 60 A.D., written that he strived to preach the Gospel, not where Christ was named. In the 100 chapters that Paul wrote he never mentions anything concerning Peter being in or around Rome, nor did any other of the New Testament writers. Just before the Roman Government executed Paul in Rome 66 A.D., he writes (2 Tim. 4:6-11): "For I am now ready to be offered, and the time of my departure is at hand. I have fought a good fight, I have finished my course, I have kept the faith," and in verse 11, "only Luke is with me." Here this great warrior, having faithfully proclaimed the Gospel in many lands and under perilous conditions for many years, longs to have fellowship and to be able to give Timothy a last farewell. Surely he would not have said, "only Luke is with me," if Peter were there in Rome. If Peter were within 500 miles he would have gone to Rome to be with Paul. But even more, the Romish Church says Peter and Paul were occupants of the same cell for several years in Rome together.

41

CHAPTER THREE

The Acts of the Popes

The contrast is great between the Acts of the Apostles, found naturally, in both the Catholic and Protestant Bibles, and the acts of the Popes, many stories of whom I cannot print, not wanting to soil the pages of this book. Then too, many large volumes could be written on the subject, but the following will suffice.

I was in an audience with the Pope, together with many others, five months ago. I was completely surprised to hear the message of the Pope which was far beneath that which would be expected from one in such a man-exalted position. Very slight mention was made of the Bible or Bible admonition, but his speech was concerning the blasphemous title, "Mother of God." The same is true of sermons made by priests. Many times I have had friendly talks with Catholics, and when they could not withstand the Scriptures, they would belittle the Bible and boast, saying that it was the Catholic Church that preserved the Scriptures during the dark ages. That is true and fine, but God uses "the wrath of man to praise Him." In fact He used a donkey to rebuke a prophet. Since they preserved the Bible, why do they not stay with the Bible and champion the Bible as do the Protestants?

One of the early fathers of the Church, Jerome (340-420) wrote: "As we accept those things that are written [in the Bible], so we reject those things which are not written [in the Bible]." ("Infallibility of the Church," page 147, E. P. Dutton & Co.)

St. Chrysostom (347-407) wrote: "Ignorance of the

Scriptures; from this it is that the plagues of heresies have broken out." ("Nicene and Post Nicene Fathers", Chas. Scribners Sons).

While I was in Rome, another experience struck me forcibly. I visited the Castle St. Angelo, that is about a mile from the Vatican and which is connected with the Vatican by a high wall. On top of it is a roadway over which the Pope would flee in time of danger. I saw the torture chamber and the air-tight chamber where a Cardinal, who had dared to question the Pope on doctrinal points, was practically smothered for two hours, and then led to the guillotine and to his death. The official Roman Catholic guide showed me the various apartments of the Popes and to my surprise, he showed me the apartments of their mistresses. He sadly expressed hope that their modern Popes were better. Everyone knows, however, about the long love affair of the late Pope with his housekeeper, who in many ways dominated the Pope, as Catholics themselves admit. How then can you expect anything less from priests and their housekeepers, and female penitents? A source of all this started with Pope Gregory VII, in 1074. We read in the Catholic Encyclopedia (Robert Appleton Co., New York) volume VI, page 794, when this Pope demanded, among other things, the divorcing of married priests, I quote, "The whole body of the married [Roman] clergy offered the most resolute resistance, and declared that the cannon enjoining celibacy was wholly unwarranted in Scripture. In support of their position they appealed to the words of the Apostle Paul, 1 Cor. 7:2, 9: "It is better to marry than to be burnt"; and 1 Tim. 3:2: "It behoveth therefore a bishop to be blameless, the husband of one wife." They cited the words of Christ, Matt. 19:11: "All men take not this word, but they to whom it is given."

43

("And I say unto you, Whosoever shall put away his wife, except it be for fornication, and shall marry another, committeth adultery: and whoso marrieth her which is put away doth commit adultery.")

This Pope Gregory would not listen to reason or the Scriptures, and has thereby brought about, through the centuries, the most horrible accumulation of corruption, crime and wickedness that the world has ever known, and has dragged with him into hell, the lives of countless millions through the transgression of God's law. But this was not all. We read on the same page that King Henry was excommunicated and his kingdom was therefore going to be taken from him by the Pope. I quote, "Abandoned by his own partisans and fearing for his throne, Henry fled secretly with his wife and child and a single servant to Gregory to tender his submission. He crossed the Alps in the depth of one of the severest winters on record. On reaching Italy, the Italians flocked around him promising aid and assistance in his quarrel with the Pope, but Henry spurned their offers. Gregory was already on his way to Augsburg, and, fearing treachery, retired to the castle of Canossa. Thither Henry followed him, but the pontiff, mindful of his former faithlessness, treated him with extreme severity. Stript of his royal robes, and clad as a penitent, Henry had to come barefooted mid ice and snow, and crave for admission to the presence of the Pope. All day he remained at the door of the citadel, fasting and exposed to the inclemency of the wintry weather, but was refused admission. A second and a third day he was thus humiliated and disciplined himself, and finally on 28 January, 1077, he was received by the pontiff and absolved from censure, but only on condition that he would appear at the proposed council and submit himself to its decision." How

44

different are the words of Jesus in answer to Peter's question, "How oft shall my brother sin against me, and I forgive him? till seven times? Jesus saith unto him, I say not unto thee, Until seven times: but Until seventy times seven." Matt. 17:21, 22. Also in 1 John 1:9, "If we confess our sins, he is faithful and just to forgive us our sins, and to cleanse us from all unrighteousness."

Bishop Strossmayer in his great speech against Papal Infallibility before the Pope and the Council of 1870, tells of some of the Papal contradictions (page 177, "The Rise and Fall of the Roman Catholic Church").

"Well, venerable brethren, here history raises its voice to assure us that some Popes have erred. You may protest against it or deny it, as you please, but I will prove it. Pope Victor (192) first approved of Montanism, and then condemned it. Marcellinus (296-303) was an idolator. He entered into the temple of Vesta, and offered incense to the goddess. You will say that it was an act of weakness; but I answer, a vicar of Jesus Christ dies rather than become an apostate. Liberius (358) consented to the condemnation of Athanasius, and made a profession of Arianism, that he might be recalled from his exile and reinstated in his see. Honorius (625) adhered to Monthelitism: Father Gratry has proven it to demonstration. Gregory I (785-90), calls any one Antichrist who takes the name of Universal Bishop, and contrary-wise Boniface III (607-9), made the parricide Emperor Phocas confer that title upon him. Paschal II (1088-99) and Eugenius III (1145-53) authorized duelling; Julius II (1509) and Pius IV (1506) forbade it. Eugenius IV (1432-39) approved of the Council of Basle and the restitution of the chalice to the church of Bohemia. Pius II (1458)

45

revoked the concession. Hadrian II (867-872) declared civil marriages to be valid; Pius VII (1800-23) condemned them. Sixtus V (1585-90) published an edition of the Bible, and by a bull recommended it to be read; Pius VII condemned the reading of it. Clement XIV (1769-1774) abolished the order of Jesuits, permitted by Paul III, and Pius VII reestablished it. . . .

"My venerable brethren, will a Pope who establishes a bank at the gates of the temple be inspired by the Holy Spirit? Will he have any right to teach the church infallibility? You know the history of Formosus too well for me to add to it. Stephen XI caused his body to be exhumed, dressed in his pontifical robes; he made the fingers which he used for giving the benediction to be cut off, and then had him thrown into the Tiber, declaring him to be a perjurer and illegitimate. He was then imprisoned by the people, poisoned, and strangled. . . . But you will tell me these are fables not history. Fables! Go, Monsignori, to the Vatican Library and read Platina the historian of the papacy, and the annals of Baronius. (A.D. 897) . . .

"I grieve, my venerable brethren, to stir up so much filth, I am silent on Alexander VI, father and lover of Lucretia; I turn away from John XXIII (1410), who, because of simony and immorality, was deposed by the holy Ecumenical Council of Constance. . . . If you decree the infallibility of the present bishop of Rome, you must establish the infallibility of all preceding ones, without excluding any. But can you do that, when history is there establishing with a clearness equal to that of the sun, that the popes have erred in their teaching? Could you do it and maintain that avaricious, incestuous, murdering, simonical popes have been vicars of Christ? Oh, venerable brethren! to maintain such an enormity would be to betray Christ worse than Judas. It would be to throw dirt in His face."

We have all heard of such a great number of anti-popes in the Romish history, and no one seems to be able to explain how they happened to come into being. It might be well to look into the Catholic Encyclopedia (Robert Appleton Co., New York), and see what we can find. Here is one, the first John XXIII. Let us see what they have to say about him (page 434, Vol. 8). "John XXIII, anti-pope of the Pisan party (1410-15) born about 1370, died 22 of November, 1419. Cardinal Baldassare Cessa (the future anti-pope in question) was one of seven Cardinals who, in May, 1408, deserted Gregory XII (q. v.), and, with those belonging to the obedience of Benedict XIII, convened the Council of Pisa of which Cossa became the leader. Descending from a noble but impoverished Neopolitan family, he embraced in his youth a military career, but later forsook it for the service of the Church. Endowed with great energy and very talented, he studied law at Bologna, where he took his doctor's degree, and then entered the service of the papal curia. On 27 February, 1402, Boniface IX made him Cardinal-Deacon of St. Eustachius, and in the following year appointed him legate."

The strange part of this story is that this man had already been known to them, according to their words, "utterly worldly minded, ambitious, crafty, unscrupulous and immoral," when they gave him these positions in the church. It is clear that rather than he being antipope, the church leaders were antichrist — for how could godly men knowingly appoint an unscrupulous, immoral man to an office in a church, unless the whole affair was in confusion and out of fellowship with Christ, which of course it was. This future antipope succeeded in deposing the two popes they had at that time, Gregory XII of Rome and Benedict XIII of Avignon. He succeeded in elevating Pietro Philarhgi to the Papacy and crowned as Alexander V. (q. v.). After Alexander V's death in 1410, this future antipope was then elected Pope, and crowned John XXIII. For some underhanded reason, the old accusations were brought against him and he too was deposed and put in jail for about a year. After that the new Pope Martin V, made him Cardinal-Bishop of Tusculum. It would even be hard for the present Pope John XXIII to expain how the Papal succession was a fact during the reign of this antipope, when the other two were completely out of office and cut off.

Most every Catholic in Italy is familiar with the story of the Borgias, and surely every priest in the world is as well. The following is taken from "Historical Studies," Eugene Lawrence, pp. 51-54. New York: Harper & Brothers, 1876.

Caesar Borgia — "a majestic monster ruled by unbridled passions and stained with blood — now governed Rome and his father by the terror of his crimes. Every night, in the streets of the city, were found the corpses of persons whom he had murdered either for their money or for revenge; yet no one dared to name the assassin. Those whom he could not reach by violence he took off by poison. His first victim was his own elder brother, Francis, Duke of Gandia, whom Alexander loved most of all his children, and whose rapid rise in wealth and station excited the hatred of the fearful Caesar. Francis had just been appointed duke of Benevento; and before he set out for Naples there was a family party of the Borgias one evening at the papal palace, where no doubt a strange kind of mirth and hilarity prevailed. The two brothers left together, and parted with a pleasant farewell, Caesar having meantime provided four assassins to waylay his victim that very night. The next morning the duke was missing; several days passed, but he did not return. It was believed that he was murdered; and Alexander, full of grief, ordered the Tiber to be dragged for the body of his favorite child. An enemy, he thought, had made away with him. He little suspected who that enemy was.

At length a Sclavonian waterman came to the palace with a startling story. He said that on the night when the prince disappeared, while he was watching some timber on the river, he saw two men approach the bank, and look cautiously around to see if they were observed. Seeing no one, they made a signal to two others, one of whom was on horseback, and who carried a dead body swung carelessly across his horse. He advanced to the river, flung the corpse far into the water, and then rode away. Upon being asked why he had not mentioned this before, the waterman replied that it was a common occurrence, and that he had seen more than a hundred bodies thrown into the Tiber in a similar manner.

The search was now renewed, and the body of the ill-fated Francis was found pierced by nine mortal wounds. Alexander buried his son with great pomp, and offered large rewards for the discovery of his murderers. At last the terrible secret was revealed to him; he hid himself in his palace, refused food, and abandoned himself to grief. Here he was visited by the mother of his children, who still lived at Rome. What passed at their interview was never known; but all inquiry into the murder ceased, and Alexander was soon again immersed in his pleasures and his ambitious designs.

Caesar Borgia now ruled unrestrained, and preyed upon the Romans like some fabulous monster of Greek mythology. He would suffer no rival to live, and he made no secret of his murderous designs. His brother-in-law was stabbed by his orders on the steps of the palace. The wounded man was nursed by his wife and his sister, the latter preparing his food lest he might be carried off by poison, while the Pope set a guard around the house to protect his son-in-law from his son. Caesar laughed at these precautions. "What cannot be done in the noonday," he said, "may be brought about in the evening." He broke into the chamber of his brother-in-law, drove out the wife and sister and had him strangled by the common executioner. He stabbed his father's favorite, Perotto, while he clung to his patron for protection, and the blood of the victim flowed over the face and robes of the Pope.

Lucrezia Borgia rivaled, or surpassed, the crimes of her brother; while Alexander himself performed the holy rites of the church with singular exactness, and in his leisure moments poisoned wealthy cardinals and seized upon their estates. He is said to have been singularly engaging in his manners, and most agreeable in the society of those whom he had resolved to destroy. At length, Alexander perished by his own arts. He gave a grand entertainment, at which one or more wealthy cardinals were invited for the purpose of being poisoned, and Caesar Borgia was to provide the means. He sent several flasks of poisoned wine to the table, with strict orders not to use them except by his directions. Alexander came early to the banquet, heated with exercise, and called for some refreshment; the servants brought him the poisoned wine, supposing it to be of rare excellence; he drank of it freely, and was soon in the pangs of death. His blackened body was buried with all the pomp of the Roman ritual.

Scarcely is the story of the Borgias to be believed: such a father, such children, have never been known before or since. Yet the accurate historians of Italy, and the careful Ranke, unite in the general outline of their crimes. On no other throne than the temporal empire of Rome has sat such a criminal as Alexander; in no other city than Rome could a Caesar Borgia have pursued his horrible career; in none other was a Lucrezia Borgia ever known. The Pope was the absolute master of the lives and fortunes of his subjects; he was also the absolute master of their souls; and the union of these two despotisms produced at Rome a form of human wickedness which romance has never imagined, and which history shudders to describe.—*"Historical Studies," Eugene Lawrence, pp.* 51-54. *New York: Harper & Brothers*, 1876.

This is a most wicked sample of a Pope that has come to light. But there were many popes who were known to be rotten. If this is true of many of their popes what must be true of their Cardinals, Bishops, and Priests! There are things that I know personally which are too vile to put in print. Let it suffice to say that the Catholics of a section of Sao Paulo, Brazil, called Ipiranga, claim that a certain priest there, is responsible for ninety children.

Some will say that this Borgia story is not true and that it is made up by the Protestants in order to slander the Catholics. Many would believe such a claim, for it is hard to imagine how a religious person in high office could fall so low. I looked into the same Catholic Encyclopedia and to my amazement the story was admitted there. But worse yet, this Pope Alexander was the father of four illegitimate children even while he was Cardinal, the Encyclopedia admits. All the religious leaders knew this and yet they exalted him as Pope over them. No wonder the Bible, giving a perfect picture of this system in Revelation, chapters 17 and 18, calls it, "Abominations of the Earth." A good encyclopedia will give the whole truth without bias or favoritism, but not so with this Catholic Encyclopedia. It admits only certain things in the story, and only admits those things since the story was so well known. But enough is admitted to prove the veracity of the whole story, which was written by such a great and faithful writer as Ranke. In fact enough was admitted by the encyclopedia to utterly condemn the Borgias and the Church which did nothing to depose him and even elevated him as Pope. I will copy citations taken from this encyclopedia, vol. 1, pages 289-293.

On page 293, we read, "The historian of the Church has the duty to dissimulate none of the trials that the Church has had to suffer from the faults of her children, and even at times from those of her own ministers." How can you ever have confidence in a Catholic encyclodedia after this. No wonder they do not declare the whole story about the Borgias.

We read on page 289, "In his twenty-ninth year (the future Pope Alexander VI) he drew a scathing letter of reproof from Pope Pius II for misconduct in Sienna which had been so notorious as to shock the whole town and court."

Also on the same page, "Even after his ordination, in 1468, he continued his evil ways."

Again on the same page we read of him, "Towards 1470 began relations with the Roman lady, Vanozza Catanei, the mother of his four children: Juan, Caesar, Lucrezia and Jofre."

Even after this, we read on the same page, "Borgia, by a bare two-thirds majority secured by his own vote, was proclaimed Pope . . . and took the name of Alexander VI." This, they admit to the eternal shame of the Roman Catholic Church.

On page 290, we read, "Alexander continued as Pope the manner of life that had disgraced his cardinalate."

On the same page, we read, "The wedding [of his daughter, Lucrezia] was celebrated in the Vatican in the presence of the Pope, ten cardinals, and the chief nobles of Rome with their ladies; the revelries of the occasion, even when exaggerations and rumors are dismissed, remain a blot upon the character of Alexander."

On page 292, we read, "Caesar (Borgia), however, continued his infamous career of simony, extortion, and treachery."

We read on the same page, "Caesar returned towards Rome, and so great was the terror he inspired that the frightened barons fled before him."

On the following page we read, "Alexander, still hale and vigorous in his seventy-third year, and looking forward to many more years of reign, proceeded to strengthen his position by repleting his treasury in ways that were more than dubious."

Most every Catholic knows these stories, and many Catholics boast that they could tell stories that we know nothing about. I am certain that only eternity will reveal the cruelty, torture, murder, sorrow and wrecked lives that this perverted religion is responsible for.

The priests get around such a history by saying that even amongst the twelve apostles, there was a Judas — so, it can be expected that there would be false priests, bishops and popes. The Bible condemns

Judas, but the Catholic Church honors Popes who have been so corrupt. Jesus said that Judas was a devil from the beginning. He had a wicked work to do, as was prophesied of him — to betray the Lord. Were all the wicked Popes, devils from the beginning? From their history, you would gather that, all right. Did they have also, a special work to do? Well, it looks as though they did, in that by their lives, acts, and teachings, people could see if they cared to, that the whole system, from center to circumference, was not of God.

But to even bring things closer home, an acquaintance told me of a recent conversation between a Protestant relative of hers and a Roman Catholic. The Catholic said, "I would like to see the blood of Protestants flow down the streets of this city." The Protestant was rightly surprised and said, "How can you say that, we are friends and you know that I am a Protestant?" The Catholic responded, "Yes, I know, but the greater the sacrifice, the greater the reward." Since they teach Catholics from childhood on, that to kill a Protestant is to do God a service, we had better be careful how we put Catholics in public office.

While I was in Ohio recently, I was told the same story by two people at different times, of a pastor who has a Christian broadcast. Through the preaching of the Gospel, this pastor at times would have Roman Catholics tell him of their difficulties and ask for advice. One case was of a lady who implicated a priest in a scandal. The pastor would always advise all those who came to him, according to the Scripture, and would urge all to trust only in Jesus Christ for their salvation. Several times, this pastor received strange telephone calls. Once a woman called and advised the pastor never to have communications with Catholics who call

54

or write in to him. He responded that it was his God-given duty to help in any way possible, all those who came to him, and that he could not comply with her request. She then said that bodily harm could come to him or those Catholics who communicated with him. The pastor responded that surely the Catholic Church would not be guilty of such an unchristian act. The answer came that the Catholic Church was too "holy" to shed blood, but they had their agents who would. Mark you, what an outrage on human intelligence, to leave the impression that the instigators of bloodshed are innocent. This is a perfect example how they do their nefarious acts, whether to individuals or nations, and manage to keep hidden from the public.

CHAPTER FOUR

The Eternal Infallible Testimony

When we consider the slaughter of 50,000 Huguenots by the Romanists on St. Bartholomew's Day, and the millions who were satanically tortured and murdered through the "Holy" Inquisition — the Papal instigations of wars and international intrigue throughout the centuries — even in the last world war, then we can see that the Eternal writings have again proven true and faithful to the people and to the nations of the world.

It is hard to imagine how in the days of the massacre, the Romanists could be so clever as to carry out such a terrible carnage without anyone else knowing about it beforehand. If they were so clever in those days, what could they be in our day? Their complicity in the first and second world wars, past unobserved by the general public — as clever as people are supposed to be today. Things are happening in Spain, Portugal, Italy, Central and South America that would make people realize the danger that this system is in the world. But here again they cleverly hide the facts and tell us that the Catholic Church is too "holy" to do such things. But we already have seen what they mean — they are "only" the instigators of corruption even when it comes to governments and governmental officials. It is almost impossible in America, because of the grip they have on the Press, for the true situation in Latin countries to be given to the public. But why go so far? I was in a Christian Patriots meeting on July 4, 1960, in Indianapolis. The preachers spoke mostly on Gospel subjects, but of course, because of the liberty of speech — and in order to save our country from Papal domination, they spoke on the dangers of Rome. In the midst of one of the meetings, ten Catholic young men got up and hollered out and tried to break up the meeting. Though police were requested for the meeting beforehand, there were none at hand. Some of us finally succeeded in getting them out in the corridor. At last a detective came up and showed his badge. He looked like an Irishman to me, and I was suspicious of him because he was so mild with the fellows. I decided to watch this thing. Finally the police arrived and when this detective thought no one was looking, for he looked around first, he shook hands with the ringleader. But the most significant thing was that, while in the corridor, one of the fellows exclaimed, "You say that we Catholics have guns and ammunition in the basements of our churches, and that we are going to use them on you Protestants some day. You are right! that is exactly what we are going to do." Where did he get that but from the priests?

This seems to be an international as well as an eternal practice with them. I was in Brazil just before the last war broke out, that is to say, just before the United States entered into the war. The world situation seemed dark and hopeless, for Hitler was gaining everywhere. Germany was doing her best by argument and threat to persuade Brazil to become an ally of Germany, and to supply them with the much needed raw material. The Catholic Church did its best to help the same cause, as all Brazilians were aware of. Finally, in the basement of a large pro-Catholic newspaper, there was discovered a vast amount of arms and ammunition to be used in a Revolution to overthrow the Brazilian government in favor of Hitler.

Some say that Catholicism in America is different than it is in the rest of the world. Do they have two Popes, one for America and another one for the rest of the world? But I must admit that Catholicism is different here than in the rest of the world, in as much as it is here, more subtle and underhanded, and therefore more dangerous.

Speaking of subtility, in the December 21, 1959, issue of "Newsweek," under the subtitle, "As Rome sees Religion's place in the government," we read a most remarkable example of Catholic double-talk, which also clearly shows that their position still is and always has been the same. We read:

Q. How does the church construe the allegiance of an American Catholic President?

A. The Church would regard him as an American citizen and an official, bound by a sacred duty to love and serve his country, and to uphold its laws *in accordance with his conscience.* This is a moral obligation on all citizens and officials, and there is nothing specifically Catholic involved. Furthermore, to answer what may be implicit in the question, *the Catholic has no split allegiance, no dual citizenship.*"

First of all, these statements were made by the Pontifical Gregorian University professor of theology, American Jesuit, William A. Van Roo, a very clever and educated man, the best they could muster for such an opportunity to fool the people. But with all his clever double-talk, it is hard to understand how he could so clearly expose the real aims of the Romish Church. He says, a Catholic President must "uphold its laws (America's) *in accordance with his conscience.*"

58

Then he says, in an attempt to cover this dangerous point, which is most likely to give himself away, he says, the same is true of any man of other religions. If this man were not so clever and well-educated, you would take him to be as ignorant as an hottentot, because of his statements. He knows, as well we all do, that no president has the right or authority to uphold the laws *in accordance with his own conscience*, but by the Constitution and laws of the land. The President, if he is not an usurper of authority, will have nothing to do with the interpretation of the Constitution or laws, there is a Judicial department for that. But he knows that the President has more power than any ruler in the world, and that if he is Catholic, he is bound to let his Roman Catholic conscience direct him wherever he can, underhandedly if necessary, openly if possible, even if it goes against the Constitution or laws of our fair land. A hundred years ago, England would not allow a Catholic to hold public office, because of the natural foreign allegiance. Two hundred years ago Sweden drove all the Catholics from their land for the same reason, but there are 360,-000 Catholics who have flooded that land, only since the last war; thanks to the apparent Roman Catholic agency for Displaced Persons. The Jesuit says, "The Catholic has no split allegiance, no dual citizenship." Here again, he tells the truth about themselves, but attempting to obscure the truth in double-talk. What fools they think we are! Lincoln was right when he said, "You can fool some of the people some of the time, but you cannot fool all the people all the time." "Father" H. S. Phelan, who was former dean of papal editors in the United States, wrote in the "Western Watchman" of St. Louis, June 27, 1912:

"Tell us that we think more of the Church than

we do of the United States; of course we do. Tell us we are Catholics first and Americans afterwards; of course we are. Tell us, in the CONFLICT BETWEEN THE CHURCH AND THE CIVIL GOVERNMENT WE TAKE THE SIDE OF THE CATHOLIC CHURCH; of course we do. Why, if the government of the United States were at war with the Church we would say tomorrow, to H—— with the government of the United States." The above words of this priest in high office speak more eloquently than I could as to the "dual citizenship" or "split allegiance," or of the Catholic duty to uphold the Constitution of the United States, or of any other country.

A remarkable statement came out in the Newsweek, April 18, 1960. "The Pope himself brought a note of alarm with a speech to the Italian Union of Catholic Jurists which called for 'necessary limitations in the exercise of the freedom of the press.' Other Popes had scored excessive abuses by the press, but none," continues the article, "had gone so far as to suggest a form of legal censorship." We all agree that former Popes were dead set against our great liberties, but according to the words of this Pope, he tops them all. If any religion cannot stand up under fire, it is not worth the powder to blow it up. Only a crook or a fake is afraid of the liberty of press or of speech. Why do they deliberately place themselves in such a category?

Pope John XXIII, wrote in the Tablet, January 9, 1960, "Today as yesterday, the Church loudly affirms that its rights and those of the family (also under its subjection) take precedence over those of the state." This statement and the one above prove that the spirit of the Catholic Church is the same as it has ever been, even through the terrible Inquisition. All that is now

60

lacking to bring about a similar, if not worse, situation than is found in Portugal, Spain, Italy and Latin America, is for them to gain the upper hand in America. Some will say that such cannot be possible, for the Protestants are in the majority; but even with religious dictators, it is the minority who enslave the majority (a late Cardinal in Spain proposed the opening of another Inquisition). They feel that if America falls, they can then strengthen their position throughout the world and then dictate in a way which would make Hitler and Stalin look like Sunday School boys. These two modern dictators could never come up to the fury of the old Inquisition. What about a modern one? Remember, history could repeat itself, if we are not careful.

We would not object if a Catholic were in public office, if it were just like any other religion, and not a foreign power as well, like the foreign Papal State, which is also bent on world domination and subjection. The great Brazilian statesman, Ruy Barbosa, who gave Brazil her Constitution, said, "Catholicism is not primarily a religion but a political body, and the most unscrupulous, and the most deadly of all political bodies."

A professor friend of mine, of a Christian college, was told by his two Catholic uncles, "Some day we will either have a Catholic President or Vice-President. If we have a Vice-President we will bump the President off and then you will find out something." It will surprise many to learn that Abraham Lincoln was assassinated by a Roman Catholic and that all those in that terrible conspiracy were either Catholic or Catholic taught. (The Rise and Fall of the Roman Catholic Church).

The Catholics have practically taken over in the

state of Rhode Island, Boston, Akron and in many other cities, and whenever they do, they arrange as soon as possible, to have the Protestants replaced by Catholics in office.

It will surprise many to learn that the more honest and upright a Catholic appears to be, the more likely he is to obey the voice of his church, even if it goes against the Constitution, for he feels he is thereby serving God.

I asked a Catholic recently if he owed his first allegiance to the United States. He responded, "Yes," but," he added, "I would obey my church if it told me to do something contrary to my country." They will all say the same thing, unless they are trying to fool people while they are running for office. Some churches have failed but not as miserably as the Roman Catholic Church, therefore a church in itself cannot altogether be trusted. Such a statement of this Catholic is giving first allegiance to a foreign power, since the Papal State and Romanism come indivisibly under the same banner. If he had said he would go against his country if it had asked him to do something contrary to the Bible, then no one would blame him. But no country will ask a person to go against the Bible (unless that country is priest-ridden or Communistic) for the Bible says that governments are ordained of God. The Bible says render therefore unto Caesar the things that are Caesar's and unto God, the things that are God's."

The web is laid, we are warned not to set foot on it. But we look at the masterpiece and think that surely it would be all right to walk on its beautiful silken and colorful surface just once. Then we remember what we have all learned, sometimes by hard experiences, that, "fools rush in where angels fear to tread." But the spider in the corner is such a genial and jovial person. With face beaming so radiantly and beckoning so invitingly our fears subside. But we remember that Stalin also used to receive flowers from little children, and fondle them and pat them on the cheeks, as he so fatherly smiled upon them — and he is accredited with more murders than Hitler. Popes are responsible for more murders than Hitler, Stalin and Nero all together. The Jesuits doctrine is, "The end justifies the means." No country, outside of Communistic or priest-ridden countries, would subscribe to such — much less the Bible.

A hypocrite is an extremely dangerous person, and is oftimes capable of anything. The more he portrays the image of a saint, the more dangerous he can be. The following is like straw thrown into the air which indicates the direction of the wind. It was written by John W. Sweetland of Royal Oak, Michigan, as printed in the Time magazine of January 4, 1960, and is as follows:

Sirs:

Re. Pope John's talk with President Eisenhower (Dec. 14, 1960). It is regrettable that the Papacy, while concerned with the suppression of the freedom of worship behind the Iron Curtain, overlooks the suppression of the same freedom in many areas of Italy, Spain, and South America, where Protestants are denied the right of free worship by the same institution that professes concern for this most sacred freedom. John W. Sweetland." A priest once said, "America will awake after it is too late." This satanic prophecy can only be fulfilled if America fails to arise now and resist this monster in every way and with all her might.

As clear as all this is, there is no better place to

find the truth of the matter, more certainly, than in the Bible, the Eternal, Infallible Testimony. Let us turn to the book of Revelation, chapters seventeen and eighteen, using either the Catholic or Protestant version of the Bible.

The seventeenth chapter deals with the end time and, as the first verse reads, "Come hither; I will show unto thee the judgment of the great whore that sitteth upon many waters."

That no one will say I have put my own interpretation to these two chapters, I will only call attention to interesting points and facts and leave the interpretation to the honest reader.

In the third verse it tells of "a scarlet colored beast, full of names of blasphemy, having seven heads and ten horns." First of all, the favorite color of Rome is scarlet. Secondly "full of names of blasphemy." You could never find a more complete set of blasphemous titles than those given to the Pope, for example, the one that belongs only to Jesus, they give to the Pope, "King of kings and Lord of lords."

The fourth verse gives the other favorite color of Rome, purple. It also tells of the "gold and precious stones and pearls." I do not think there is a larger collection of gold and precious stones and pearls, than in the Vatican.

The sixth verse tells of the "woman drunk with the blood of the saints." No organization, nation or group of nations has been responsible for the death of more Christians than has Papal Rome.

In the seventh verse, it refers to a beast "which hath seven heads and ten horns." Then in verse nine it explains these. "The seven heads are seven mountains on which the woman sitteth." Everybody knows that Rome is built on seven mountains, and too that the old Roman Empire consisted of ten nations, as the Bible affirms.

Then in the fifteenth verse we read, "The waters which thou saweth, where the whore sitteth, are peoples, and multitudes, and nations, and tongues." In history there is no organization or group of nations that have spread itself throughout the world as has Papal Rome. Some proudly say, "Our Catholic Church is the largest in the world." According to the words of Jesus, that is a fact to be shunned rather than to be boasted of. We read His words in Matthew 7:13, "Enter ye at the strait gate: for wide is the gate, and broad is the way, that leadeth to destruction, and *many there be which go in thereat*: Because strait is the gate, and *narrow is the way, which leadeth unto life, and few there be that find it.*"

But another clear point in the chapter is the last verse, "and the woman which thou sawest is that great city, which reigneth over the kings of the earth." Every school child knows that it is Rome which has ruled over the kings of the earth.

But what I like about these two chapters and the subject as a whole, (and this is the reason that this book has been written) is in the loving and faithful words of our Lord (Rev. 18:4), "Come out of her, my people, that ye be not partakers of her sins, and that ye receive not of her plagues."

CHAPTER FIVE

The Great Conspiracy or
The Murder of Abraham Lincoln

This chapter will be given to citations from the great book, "Rome's Responsibility for the Assassination of Abraham Lincoln" by Thomas M. Harris, the late Brigadier General U. S. V.

We will start, however with the prefatory note, written by J. D. Williams, in Pittsburgh, Pa., June 17, 1897, which is interesting:

"General Harris needs no word of introduction from me; and yet it may not be amiss to detain the reader just a moment with some allusion to the General's eminent adaptability to do the work which he has so nobly performed in this unpretentious volume. The author passes his 84th "mile stone" today. He has been a painstaking student and careful observer of the teachings and practices of Romanism. He knows his subject fully along the lines of historical Romanism. And being a member of the "Military Commission" that tried and condemned the conspirators he had unusual opportunities for accurate knowledge concerning Rome's responsibility for the "Crime of the Ages" — the assassination of Abraham Lincoln. And he has here presented a chain of evidence which ought to result in the expulsion of the *Jesuits* from American soil.

"The book deserves to be read and pondered by every American freeman.

"I cannot better close this note than in the words of Lincoln himself. In 1864 he said:

" 'If the American people could learn what I know of the fierce hatred of the priests of Rome against our institutions, our schools, our most sacred rights, and our so dearly bought liberties, they would drive them out as traitors.' "

We now quote a part of the Publisher's Forword of this book reprinted in 1960. (Heritage Manor, P. O. Box 75673, Stanford Station, Los Angeles 5, California)

"Let America again be forewarned as to Rome's intention 'to make America Catholic.' Assassination is an approved method of the Church of Rome to gain her ends. In a letter to Nuncio Sega, Madrid, December 12, 1580, Pope Gregory XII said:

" 'Since that guilty woman (Queen Elizabeth I) of England rules over two such noble Kingdoms of Christendom, and is the cause of so much injury to the Catholic faith, and loss of so many millions of souls, there is no doubt that whosoever sends her out of the world with the pious intention of doing God service, not only does not sin but gains merit, especially having regard to the sentence pronounced against her by Pius V of holy memory.'

"That was in 1580. Now, we turn to the year 1938:

"Heresy is an awful crime against God, and those who start a heresy are more guilty than they who are traitors to the civil government. If the state has a right to punish treason with death, the principle is the same that concedes to the spiritual authority (Roman Catholic Church) the power of life and death over the archtraitor." THE TABLET (Catholic Weekly), November 5, 1938.

"Popes have been consistent in their declarations that freedom of religion should NOT exist, and that the Church of Rome represents the only true faith and therefore should alone be allowed to spread its doctrines.

"In a Catholic state liberty of conscience and religion must be understood according to Catholic doctrine and Catholic law." Pope Pius XI, April 30, 1939.

"A predecessor of Pius XI said: 'In truth, the (Catholic) Church judges it not lawful that the various kinds of Divine Worship should have the same right as the true religion. . . . Wherefore, it is evident there is just cause for Catholics to undertake the conduct of public affairs . . .to infuse into ALL the veins of the commonwealth the wisdom and virtue of the Catholic Church.' Pope Leo XIII, encyclical Christian Constitution of States."

Later in the forword we read:

"Pope John XXIII said today that the rights of the Roman Catholic Church in the teaching of youth come before the rights of the State." THE CITIZEN-NEWS, Los Angeles, December 31, 1959.

"ALL baptized persons are subject to the laws of the (Catholic) Church." Canon 87, Woywod & Smith in PRACTICAL COMMENTARY ON THE CODE OF CANON LAW.

On page seven, we read the words of the Brigadier General: "Is there no danger when the Roman Hierarchy quarters its wily agents in the capital of our nation to exert their influence in shaping our laws, and in controlling Presidential appointments to the highest and most important offices? Is there not *danger when all our politicians who aspire to national fame feel that in order to succeed they must truckle to Rome, and be submissive?* Is there not danger when the capital of our nation has been captured by the wily *Jesuit,* and Washington is literally 'in the lap of Rome?' Go into any and all of the departments of our government and find *seven elevenths* of the government employees in several of them, adject slaves of the Pope, and tell me is there no danger? Go into all of our cities and larger towns and find our municipal governments in the hands of the faithful *servants of* this foreign despot, *the Pope,* and who *are corruptly administering their affairs to enrich the church at the expense of the people,* and tell me, is there no danger? Contemplate *this alien* and *dangerous power in complete control of three-fourths of our newspapers* and periodicals, and tell me, is there no danger? Look at this alien organization levying tribute continually on Protestant business men all over the land, and growing rich on tribute thus levied, and secured through fear of the boycott and then tell me, if you can, that there is no danger? *Look at the Protestant pulpit, for the most part muzzled and dumb through fear of the boycott against their members who are engaged in business, and on whom they largely depend for their salaries,* and then tell me if you can, that there is no danger."

We read on page 9:

"What does it mean that a systematic process of procuring arms and ammunitions is being put into operation?

"What does it mean that the basements of churches, cathedrals, and school buildings are being converted into arsenals, in which to store away arms and munitions of war? Does it not indicate a *purpose,* if need be, in the struggle for supremacy, to resort to revolution and bloodshed?

"Is it a mere happen so, that the rank and file in the army of the United States is made up, very largely, of the subjects of this foreign potentate, the Pope of Rome, men who from their childhood have been taught implicit obedience to his authority as the price of the salvation of their souls, and who, in a conflict of authority between the Pope and the government of the United States, would, without hesitation, yield allegiance to the Pope?

Is it not a fact worthy of some thought that a very undue proportion of the field and line officers in our army are members of this church, and that the same state of things is found in our navy? Is it not a fact that demands our attention that a largely undue proportion of the cadets in our military schools are members, by birth, baptism, and confirmation, of the Roman Catholic Church?

"Do not these very significant and important facts clearly indicate that there is an unseen power holding watch and guard over, and controlling these things?"

On page ten we read:

"*Two-thirds of the enlisted men on duty at West Point*, and five of the officers there in command, and the family of a sixth, *are* members of the Roman Catholic Church. The only use I now intend to make of this reference is simply to ask the question, 'How does it come about that Rome has gotten such a hold in our army?' Is it a purely accidental thing that five of the officers and two-thirds of the enlisted men on duty at this Military School of the United States Government, are Roman Catholics?"

We read on page 12, of an interesting and startling bit of history by this high-ranking officer who was an eye witness:

"It was the Pope of Rome, and his faithful lieutenant, Louis Napoleon, who, taking advantage of our civil war, undertook to establish a Roman Catholic empire in Mexico, and for this purpose sent Maximilian, a Roman Catholic prince, under the protection

70

of a French army, to usurp dominion, and take possession of the country. All of this was done in the hope that the Union cause would be lost; and that through the strife that she had fomented, two Roman Catholic empires would be established on the American continent, viz. that of Mexico under Maximilian and that of the Confederacy under Jefferson Davis; thus making it possible to make a conquest of the entire continent. This letter of the Pope to Jefferson Davis, couched in such courteous and loving terms, and showing so clearly that his sympathy was with the Southern cause, was well understood by his loyal and faithful subjects all over the North. Roman Catholic officers began to resign and the rank and file began to desert, from the time of the publication of that letter in 1863 to the close of the war.

"In reply to the boast so freely made by Roman Catholic editors and orators that the Irish fought the battles of the civil war and saved the nation, the following document, received from the Pension department at Washington, is here given:

Whole number of troops	2,128,200
Natives of the United States	1,627,267
Germans	180,817
Irishmen	144,221
British (other than Irish)	90,040
Other foreigners and missions	87,855

The "Desertions" were as follows:

Natives of the United States	5%
Germans	10%
Irish Catholics	72%
British (other than Irish)	7%
Other foreigners	7%

"In other words: of the 144,000 Irishmen that enlisted, 104,000 deserted. And it is reliably stated that most of these desertions occurred after the recognition of the Confederacy by the Pope. It is also a fact that of the five percent of native Americans rated as deserters, 45 percent of the 5 percent were Catholics. —TOLEDO AMERICAN, as quoted on page 115 of "Why Am I An A. P. A."

"This is a sufficient proof of the charge heretofore made, that a good Roman Catholic can only be loyal to the Pope; and so can never be loyal to our government, and to our Protestant institutions.

"It is true that there were some able and brave Roman Catholic officers in the Union army, who were truly loyal to the cause; as also many in the ranks who were nominally members of the Roman Catholic Church; but these were they who had been *educated in our free schools*, and had thus become so *imbued with the American Spirit, that they were no longer good Catholics.* All honor to these!

"Not only by desertions and resignations was Roman Catholic disloyalty made apparent, but more conspicuously by the draft riots that followed, the rioters being made up, almost entirely, of Irish Roman Catholics. Arch-bishop Hughes *posed* as a Union man; and was so far trusted by President Lincoln, that he solicited his good offices at Rome, to prevent the Pope from giving recognition to the Confederate government; he being well aware of the consequences that would follow such recognition. The Arch-bishop proved a traitor to his trust; and the Pope's letter to Jefferson Davis followed closely on the heels of his visit to Rome, and resignations and desertions commenced. Then followed the terrible riots in New York City, when a draft became necessary to fill up our depleted ranks. For three fearful days and nights the city was terrorized by the violence of an Irish Catholic mob, right un-

72

der the shadow of the Arch-bishop's palace. The Arch-bishop kept secluded in his palace, and as mute as a mouse, until notified by Mr. Lincoln that he would be held personally responsible for its continuance. He then came forth; and by a few kind words to the rioters, whom he addressed as his friends, the mob immediately dispersed, and order was restored. It only took a few words from him to accomplish what could not have been accomplished without much bloodshed, and perhaps the destruction of the city, by a military army of our government; but mark! those words were not spoken until it became necessary to the personal safety of the Arch-bishop. The traitor was here revealed. And now we come to the last desperate conspiracy to overthrow our government, and make the rebellion a success by a resort to *the favorite policy of the Jesuits, that of assassination.*"

"I do not propose to affirm or deny the charge that is now being commonly and openly made by patriotic papers and lectures, that Rome was responsible for the assassination of our martyred President, but simply to present the facts, and leave my readers to draw their conclusion from a consideration of the facts in the case. My own personal convictions will no doubt be made obvious before I get through. The very fact that the charge is being made by a high class of men, men noted for intelligence, patriotism and uprightness of character, justifies us in making a careful scrutiny of the evidence on which it rests; that we may fairly judge whether or not it has been justly made. It is a charge of too much gravity and of too serious an import to be made lightly, or on insufficient grounds."

"So deep, and bitter, was their disappointment at the signal success of the government in the vindication of its authority, and its right to exist, that for a quarter of a century it never ceased its efforts to fix upon it the stigma of this alleged crime, and it was only e-stopped from this effort by the publication of my 'History of the Great Conspiracy' to overthrow our government by a series of assassinations, when, fearing that its further agitation might tend to give publicity to my book, and that thus the facts of this conspiracy would become more widely known, and the truth of history vindicated, that the agitation of this charge, and contention against the government was dropped as it had become a hot potato. *We must not forget, that in all this, they acted under a full knowledge of all the facts in the case.* These had been fully displayed to the world through the evidence produced by the government on the trial of the assassins in 1865, and two years later, still more fully, on the trial of John H. Surratt in a civil court. These things were not done in a corner, but openly before the world. Their sympathy with the conspirators and assassins, and their enmity toward the government, was thus openly proclaimed before the world; and the attitude of the Hierarchy toward the assassination of the nation's head, was clearly manifest. It was Abraham Lincoln, it is true, that was slain, but it was the life of the nation that the blow was aimed at. The scheme to aid the rebellion by the assassination of the President, the Vice-President, the Secretary of State, the Secretary of War, and the General in command of our armies, was concocted by the emissaries of the rebel government, who kept their headquarters in Montreal, Canada. These emissaries held a semi-official relation to the Confederate government. The whole run of the evidence makes it clear that the Roman Hierarchy kept itself in close relations with these emissaries; and it is highly probable, from a consideration of all of the facts, with the head of the government in whose service they were employed also. It kept itself in these close relations for a purpose, and was most likely the original source of the inspiration of the assassination plot."

On page twenty-one, we read a most revealing story of Papal and priestly deceit:

"The *Jesuit* plans with the utmost art and cunning, unhampered by any moral restraints, and always with the utmost secrecy; and carries out his plans in the dark. We think, however, that in this case, we have succeeded in tracing him through all the devious wanderings of his dark and slimy path, and, in fixing upon him the responsibility for the assassination of President Lincoln.

"But we are not done yet. In the early part of September, 1865, these unholy Fathers thought it safe to unload their charge onto their brethren in England; and so made arrangements for sending Surratt across the Atlantic, under an assumed name, and in disguise.

. . .

"They had consigned him to the care of their friends in Liverpool, by the hands of Dr. McMillen, and through whose aid Surratt succeeded in placing himself under the care of the Roman Catholic Church in a foreign land. Rome is everywhere, and always the same, and he can feel safe as long as he is in the custody of the church. Here he waited for the Peruvian to make another voyage to Quebec and return. He sent by the surgeon, to his rebel employers in Canada, a request to send him some money; but only to receive the answer that they had no money for him. The expense of sending him across the continent, to Italy, thus fell on the church. His rebel friends had now forsaken him; but the church stood by him. He was sent to Italy and was mustered into the army of the

Pope. Here he remained safely hidden away for a year or more; but was finally discovered by a government detective who had been sent in search of him, and who went voluntarily, hoping to get the offered reward, and who had enlisted in the same company to which Surratt belonged. This detective informed our government of his discovery; and through the agents of our government the Pope was informed that his soldier, who had enlisted under the name of Watson, was none other than the notorious John H. Surratt, who was a member of the conspiracy that accomplished the assassination of President Lincoln.

"With a shrewd show of virtuous innocence, the Pope hastened to clear his skirts, and those of his underlings, by ordering his arrest, and rendition to our government, without waiting for its requisition. He was arrested by the Pope's authority, but was allowed to escape by his guards; and thus given another chance for life and liberty. The story was, that he made his escape by a bold leap over a precipice, at the risk of his life. 'Tell this to the marines; the old sailors will not believe it.' He was finally captured at Alexandria, Egypt, and was brought home in chains, where he was held to answer for his crime. Let us here pause a moment to consider the relations of the Hierarchy to this crime.

"The testimony given on the trial of John H. Surratt, clearly convicts two of its priests, Boucher and LaPierre, of being accomplices in the conspiracy; and by implication, as clearly convicts the Bishop of Montreal, Bishop Bourget. This testimony was spread before the world, and so must have been known to the Roman Catholic Hierarchy, yet it never called any of these priests to accountability, or held them responsible for this crime; the crime of the ages! No one of them

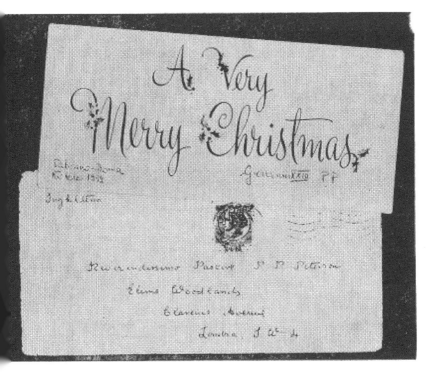

A Christmas card sent to the author from Pope, John XXIII, after he sent him a copy of his book, "The Rise and Fall of the Roman Catholic Church." He sent the card (instead of to the author's business address) to the author's home address while in England, which he thought no one knew of. In other words the Pope was saying, "We have got your number."

March 15, 1960,
3271 - 41 Street,
Astoria, L: I.,
New York.

Father P. B. Bagatti,
Tipografia PP. Franciscani,
Jerusalem, Jordon.

Dear Reverend Bagatti:

I have just returned from a wonderful
trip to Europe and the Holy Land, but I
believe that the most outstanding event to
me was the learning of the great discovery
of the ancient Christian burial ground, there
on the Mount of Olives at your monastery,
"Dominus Flevit". I have spoken with a
number of Franciscan priests and monks, and
they have told me about you and the book you
are co-writer of. I had hoped to meet you
and to compliment you on such a great discovery, but time would not permit. Having
heard so much about you, and that you are an
archeologist, I was very much convinced with
you, concerning the ancient Christian burial
ground and that the remains found in the bone
box with the name on it, "Simon Bar Jona",
written in Aramaic, were those of St. Peter.

One thing I did not get straight, altogether; was it the Franciscans who really
were the first to make the discovery of the
Tomb of St. Peter and the ancient Christian
burial ground?

If you ever come to New York, I would
be very glad to meet you, and if possible to
have lunch with you.

Hoping to hear from you soon,
I am,
Very sincerely yours,

F. Paul Peterson

The above is a letter the author sent to the well-known
archeologist and priest, P. B. Bagatti.

STUDIUM BIBLICUM FRANCISCANUM

JERUSALEM

Jerusalem, Flagellatio 28 Marzo '60

Ill.mo Signore.

Grazie della sua lettera.Le lettura "bar Jona" è mia,però nella relazione definitiva dello scavo ho lasciato ad uno specialista,J.T.Milik la cura di pubblicare le iscrizioni.Egli(p.83) dice che in questa lettura "resta possibile,ma si può proporre altri egualmente verisimili".

Ammesso pure che sia "Jona" come io credo,può essere qualche parente di S.Pietro,dal momento che i nomi si tramandano nelle famiglie.Per poter proporre l'identificazione con S.Pietro bisogna andar contro una lunga tradizione,che ha il suo valore.Ad ogni modo un prossimo volume dimostrerà che tutto il cimitero é cristiano e del I-II secolo d.C.

La saluto in Domino

devotissimo

P. B. Bagatti
OFM

The above is the letter, in Italian, from Priest Bagatti
in answer to the author's letter.

This is the envelope, from Jerusalem, in which
Priest Bagatti sent his letter to the author.

was ever held to have forefeited his standing or good character in the church, on account of his connection with this conspiracy; and so, the Hierarchy stands before the world today, as having given its approval to their conduct in this matter."

Now we give you an account which freedom-loving, open-hearted and honest people can hardly understand. But this is a perfect example of the Romish spirit in all her history, which bears out the Jesuit motto, "The end justifies the means." We read on page twenty-seven:

"It would seem that the *Jesuits* had had it in mind, from the beginning of the war, to find an occasion for the taking off of Mr. Lincoln. Early in the war, they set a paragraph going the rounds of the press, as far as they had it under their control, to the effect that Mr. Lincoln had been born in the Catholic Church, and had been made a member of the church by his baptism into it, and that he had apostatized, and became a heretic. Mr. Lincoln had seen this statement going the rounds of the press, and believed that such a gross falsehood would not have been published without a purpose. On the occasion of a visit from Father Chiniquy about this time, Mr. Lincoln called his attention to this paragraph, saying, he had been greatly perplexed in trying to discover the object of its publication; and asking him if he could give any clue to the motive that had inspired such a falsehood. I will give Father Chiniquy's own account of his interview with the President on this subject.

" 'The next day, I was there at the appointed hour, with my noble friend, who said, "I could not give you more than ten minutes yesterday, but I will give you twenty today: I want your views about a thing which is exceedingly puzzling to me, and you are the only one to whom I like to speak on that subject. A great number of Democratic papers have been sent to me, lately, evidently written by Roman Catholics, publishing that I was born a Roman Catholic; and baptized by a priest. They call me a renegade, an apostate, on account of that; and they heap upon my head mountains of abuse. At first, I laughed at that, for it is a lie, thanks be to God, I have never been a Roman Catholic. No priest of Rome has ever laid his hand on my head. But the persistency of the Romish press to present this falsehood to their readers as a gospel truth, must have a meaning: Please tell me, as briefly as possible what you think about that.' "My dear President'" I answered, 'it was just this strange story published about you, which brought me here yesterday. I wanted to say a word to you about it; but you were too busy.

" 'Let me tell you that I wept like a child when I read that story for the first time. For, not only my impression is, that it is your sentence of death, but I have it from the lips of a converted priest, that it is in order to excite the fanaticism of the Roman Catholic murderers, whom they hope to find, sooner or later, to strike you down, they have invented that false story of your being born in the church of Rome, and of your being baptized by a priest. They want by that to brand your face with the ignominious mark of apostacy. Do not forget that, in the church of Rome, an apostate is an outcast, who has no place in society, and who has no right to live. The *Jesuits* want the Roman Catholics to believe that you are a monster, an open enemy of God and of the church, that you are an excommunicated man. I have brought to you the theology of one of the most learned and approved of the *Jesuits* of his time, Bussambaum, who, with many others, say that the man who will kill you, will do a good and holy work. More than that, here is a copy of a decree of Gregory VII, proclaiming that the killing of an apostate, or a heretic, and an excommunicated man, as you are declared to be, is not murder, nay, that it is a good, a christian action. That decree is incorporated in the canon law, which every priest must study, and which every good Catholic must follow.

" 'My dear President, I must repeat to you here, what I said in Urbanna, in 1856. My fear is that you will fall under the blows of a *Jesuit assassin*, if you do not pay more attention than you have done, till now, to protect yourself. Remember that because Coligny was a heretic, as you are, he was brutally murdered in the St. Bartholomew night; that Henry IV was stabbed by the *Jesuit assassin*, Revaillae, the 14th of May, 1610, for having given liberty of conscience to his people, and that William, the Taciturn, was shot dead by another Jesuit murderer, called Girard, for having broken the yoke of the Pope. The *church of Rome* is absolutely the same today, as she was then; she *does believe and teach, today,* as then, that she has the right and *that it is her duty to punish with death any heretic who is in her way as an obstacle to her designs.*

" 'The unanimity with which the Catholic Hierarchy of the United States is on the side of the rebels, is an incontrovertible evidence that Rome wants to destroy the Republic, and as you are, by your personal influence and popularity, your love of liberty, your position, the greatest obstacle to their diabolical scheme, their hatred is concentrated on you; you are the daily object of their maledictions; it is at your breast they will direct their blows. My blood chills in my veins when I contemplate the day which may come, sooner or later, when *Rome will add to all her other iniquities, the murder of Abraham Lincoln.'*

"The charge that Rome was responsible for the assassination of Abraham Lincoln was first made, so far as I am advised, by Father Chiniquy; and was founded not only on the facts which I have here given; but on facts that came to him as a result of his own personal research. His charge is distinctly and explicitly made in his book, entitled, *"Fifty Years in the Church of Rome."* He there shows that Mr. Lincoln had incurred the deadly enmity of the *Jesuits* by foiling and disappointing them in an effort they made to convict Father Chiniquy of a crime, of which they had falsely accused him; and which, had they succeeded in convicting him, would not only have ruined his reputation, but would have secured his incarceration in a prison.

"Mr. Lincoln defended Father Chiniquy, and being furnished, apparently by a special Providence, with evidence that revealed their wicked conspiracy to destroy him, and convicted them of perjury, he was able triumphantly, to defeat their wicked scheme; and gave them such a scathing as made them tremble with rage, and slink away with vows of vengeance in their hearts."

We now quote the conclusion of the matter upon which every true, peace-loving, freedom-loving American must stand upon, on page thirty-nine:

"Our country must be maintained as it is now, the land of liberty, under the protection of Protestant institutions. Let us then declare to the world this purpose, by bringing it under the control of a 'Protestant American Party.'

"The Hierarchy has never had to encounter anything in this country that has given it so much concern as does the present patriotic awakening. It af-

84

fects, however, to regard it with contempt, but at the same time *redoubles its efforts to tighten its grasp on the politicians.* It is to them that it looks for help, and appeals for aid. It tries to hide the real issues, by its usual resort to misrepresentation and falsehood. *It represents it as a revival of know-nothingism.* In this it is not so far wrong. The A. P. A. is, however, built on a broader foundation, as a result of a wider knowledge, and more extended experience of the deadly hostility of Rome to our civil institutions; and so upon a better comprehension of the safeguards that are necessary for their protection.

"*It represents this, and all the other patriotic organizations, as founded on bigotry, and for the purpose of religious persecution; and so, as being un-American and unpatriotic. And all this is to throw chaff into the eyes, that they may be closed to the threatened danger.*

"But in this way many well meaning people and true friends of our institutions, and lovers of our country's flag, are being deceived, and lulled to sleep. Now, why does Rome resort to this line of defense? It is because all of the facts are against her, and so, as they cannot be denied or controverted, her policy is to hide them out of sight, by changing the line of vision. Rome knows, and every American citizen ought to know, that these *anti-Catholic agitators are unearthing her purposes, and uncovering her plans to get hold of all the departments of our government,* and then give to the Pope all that he claims as Christ's vicar; supreme control over our civil institutions; that he may yield the civil power for the upbuilding of the so-called church. We have only to turn to the pages of history to learn how he would use this power. We want no more of his interference with our God-given rights. We want

85

no more union of church and state; and *the danger lies more than anything else, in the seeming incredibility that there should be any persons found at this late day, and in this land of ours, who would favor a return to the rack, the thumb-screws, and other instruments of inquisition torture,* for the promotion of the glory of God, and the salvation of souls.

"Let the incredulous look at Rome's boasted declaration: *Semper eadem. (Always the same.)* Let them also scan the declarations made by Romish priests of every grade, in recent years, in the Roman Catholic Journals and Periodicals, and they will learn that all that Rome wants is the power to enable her to revive these mild methods of propagating her version of the gospel of Christ. Why doesn't she meet the charges that are made against her openly and fairly? When it is charged that she is storing away arms in the basements of her churches, why does she not proffer the keys, and invite inspection? When it is charged that she is restraining helpless females of their liberty, for the basest purposes, and inflicting upon them untold cruelties to bring them under subjection to a lecherous, drunken priesthood, why does she not open her doors, and appeal to the civil magistrates to make the most rigid inspection and examination, that they may thus show the charges to be false? This she has never yet done, and never will do; neither will she permit it to be done as long as she can find means for successful resistance.

"In the name of liberty, in the cause of humanity, let us compel her to submit to such inspections. In the name of Protestant Americanism, let us set up our banners for complete subjugation of this corrupt, unscrupulous, and dangerous foe to liberty, and murderer of human rights.

"Let it be known to the world that American freemen will ever stand on the watch tower, and will compel the submission of all within the domain of our government to submit themselves to its rightful authority. That there can be in this country in civil affairs no power greater than the State."

The following organizations are faithfully working for the enlightment of both Catholics and Protestants. They merit your whole-hearted confidence in the universal struggle against Paganism, Popery and corruption, and for the preservation of the great American liberties which are natural, and God-given human rights. Write to them for their literature.

1. American Protestant Defense League
   350 West 26th St., New York City, N. Y.

2. Christian Heritage
   Box 925, Sea Cliff, New York

3. The Convert
   P. O. Box 90, Clairton, Pa.

4. The Christian Patriots of America
   P. O. Box 92, Anderson, Indiana

Write to them for information concerning their Christian speakers who may be engaged for meetings in your church.

There is another organization which has a dedicated group of lawyers, set aside to the most necessary task of legally resisting the constant encroachments of Romanism upon our constitution. It is called, "Protestants and Others for the Separation of Church and State" (P.O.A.U.). Send for their literature and inform them immediately should you know of any such encroachments. Contact:

Mr. Glen Archer

c/o P.O.A.U.,

1633 Massachusetts St., N.W., Washington, D. C.

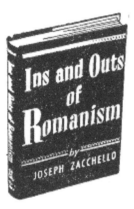

Made in United States
Cleveland, OH
20 May 2025

17050572R00056